# THE ALTERNATIVE HOLIDAY GUIDE

GW00492864

# Golfing in Europe

by

## Eric Humphreys

Ashford Press Publishing
Southampton
1989

Published by  Ashford Press Publishing
1 Church Road
Shedfield
Hampshire
SO3 2HW

*British Library Cataloguing in Publication Data*

Humphreys, Eric
  The alternative holiday guide to golfing in Europe.
  1. Europe – Visitors' guides – For golf
  I.  Title
  914'.04'5502479635
  ISBN  1-85253-106-1


Designed and set by Jordan and Jordan, Fareham, Hampshire

Printed by Hartnolls Limited, Bodmin, Cornwall, England

While great care has been taken in the compilation of this book, the
author and publisher cannot guarantee that all details, such as prices,
schedules, addresses and telephone numbers will remain unchanged
and exactly as quoted here.

The author has no connection with any business or establishment
listed here, and no guarantee or endorsement is implied or given in this
respect. That a business or establishment is *not* listed or detailed does
not imply any criticism.


*Throughout this guide course lengths are given in either metres or
yards, according to the system of measurement adopted in their design.
Individual design has also determined that some courses offer golfers a
par, whilst others prefer to give a Standard Scratch Score (SSS).*

# Contents

# Denmark

# Sweden

# France

# Belgium

# Holland

# Germany

# Italy

# List of Photographs

# List of Maps

# Foreword

It is my pleasure to write the foreword to this book and to recall some of the great golf courses in Europe that I have been privileged to play.

It seems a lifetime since my early days as an assistant professional, when I was trying to make my mark in the world of professional golf, but even in those few years there have been many changes, not only in the design of golf courses but also in golf equipment. Many of the championship courses of Europe have stood the test of time with little or no alterations to complement the changes in golf clubs and golf balls, which in itself speaks volumes for the old golf course architects.

The compulsory use of the big ball was undoubtedly a major factor in the resurgence of golf in Europe and one of the reasons why European golf is now the dominant force in the world game. Obviously, my win in the Open Championship at Royal Lytham and St Annes in 1969 comes to mind as does my win in the United States Open Championship at Chaska, Minnesota, in 1970 and there is no doubt in my mind that my early golf in Europe laid a solid foundation. I remember clearly the problems I had the night before the final round at Royal Lytham and also a message that was left on the door of my locker in Chaska by Tom Weiskopf and Bert Yancey which simply said 'Tempo'. I also recall an opening round of 67 at St Andrews in the 1970 Open when play was abandoned after violent storms and a 6 at the par 5 17th hole at Birkdale in the final round of the 1971 Open Championship which relegated me to third spot behind the winner, Lee Trevino and the runner-up, Mr Lu. But golf is like that. No respecter of persons and a great leveller.

Those bitter-sweet memories have been offset by two victories in the Ryder Cup, one at the Belfry, the other at the Jack Nicklaus-designed Muirfield Village, Ohio, USA when I had the great pleasure of being the non-playing Captain. These two victories were honed to perfection on some of the tough and demanding golf courses in Europe.

I have been privileged to make many good and true friends through golf and I am happy to have been able to share some of those heady moments with Eric Humphreys. His technical knowledge of the golf swing coupled with his love of golf has been accepted in many parts of the world and a number of world-class golfers have benefitted from his advice from time to time. His writings, both humorous and instructional reflect his longstanding involvement with the Royal and Ancient game.

I enjoyed reading the manuscript. I hope you enjoy the book, and it only remains for me to wish you many happy and successful hours on the golf courses of your choice. *The Alternative Holiday Guide to Golfing in Europe* should provide some first-class suggestions as to where to play and will be a welcome addition to your golfing library.

Tony Jacklin, OBE

# Acknowledgements

I would like to acknowledge with thanks the assistance of the following in the preparation of this book: Atalya Aparta Golf, Atlantic Golf, The French Government Tourist Office, The Gleneagles Hotel, The Irish Tourist Board (Bord Failte), Longshot Golf Holidays by Meon, Sky Golf Holidays, Sovereign Gold Golf Holidays and Venice Simplon Orient Express Hotels. I would also like to thank the following for the use of photographs: Baden Baden Golf Club (p. 147), The Danish Tourist Board (p. 95), The French Government Tourist Office (pp. 115, 127), The Gleneagles Hotel (p. 28), The Irish Tourist Board (Bord Failte) (pp. 40, 42, 45, 131), Longshot Golf Holidays by Meon (pp. 59, 60, 62, 63, 78, 79, 83, 91), The Northern Ireland Tourist Board (pp. 29, 36, 37), Phil Sheldon (pp. 155) and Venice Simplon Orient Express Hotels (pp. 11, 21).

# Introduction – The Royal and Ancient Game

The game of golf has become an international pastime involving millions of people, and the development of residential accommodation that goes hand in hand with new courses involves millions of dollars, pesetas, yen, pounds sterling – in fact every negotiable currency imaginable. Give any golf course architect the sight of a piece of seemingly useless land and in the flash of a steel-shafted golf club you have a new and sometimes exciting challenge. That row upon row of houses, bungalows, villas and apartments often line the sides of each fairway is a part of the price that one has to pay.

Whilst there is clear evidence that the game of golf as we know it today was first played in Scotland there are those who will tell you that a form of golf was played in China some 2000 years ago. It has also been said that another form of the Royal and Ancient game was played on ice, in Holland, and paintings by early Dutch and Flemish painters show men standing or skating on ice and wielding large curved clubs with a large ball lying near them.

It is, however, a fact that the first Code of Rules was put out in 1744 by the Gentlemen of Leith, Scotland. These rules numbered but thirteen and the first movement towards a uniform government of the game of golf started in 1754 when the Society of St Andrews Golfers was formed. Members of this and other similar societies often gathered at St Andrews because of the availability of the links course. The players were 'men of substance'.

The game of golf has spread so much since those early days that it is hard to realise that less than a century ago it was virtually unknown outside Scotland. The first golf course in England was at Blackheath, just outside London, and Old Manchester and Westward Ho! followed. The first permanent club in the United States was opened in 1888 at Yonkers, New York and it was not long before Europe and Japan started to build their own courses.

The first golf courses were on windswept linksland where, prior to the great golfing boom, a few holes were cut out of hitherto useless land where only a few scruffy sheep grazed. And it was these sheep that were responsible for the first natural hazards. In their efforts to shield themselves from the gale-force winds the sheep huddled in the soft ground and over the passage of time formed small depressions which were later known as bunkers. The development of golf architecture was a natural progression and as more inland sites became available even the original links courses were subject to significant change. And if the majority of the golf courses in Britain were rudimentary in layout, certainly before the 1900s, at least they existed. Golf in the rest of the world is a twentieth-century pastime.

The 1920s saw the first boom in golf course design and little of significance happened until the 1960s when another surge in course-building took place. It was during the sixties boom that property developers began to use the surrounding land on which to build villas, apartments and houses. This was especially true of Spain and Portugal where the weather was conducive to golf all the year round and in many instances, British architects were eagerly sought.

The evolution of golf clubs and golf balls followed as the golf courses became more sophisticated and holes became longer and more difficult. The first feather golf ball was obviously limited in its flight and the distance to which it could be struck. The gutta-percha ball quickly took over from the 'featherie' and it was not too long before the modern ball was designed and accepted. This golf ball has changed little since the first rubber-core ball was invented in 1898. Some had a liquid centre on which elastic was wound and the modern version which usually has a 'solid' centre has been encased in a variety of covers such as surlyn and balata. The difference in scoring with the emergence of the modern ball was dramatic when compared with its predecessors.

The new golf clubs, with their steel shafts, also played a part in the improvement in golf scores but whilst the old clubs had names like Baffie, Spoon, Driving Iron, Mid-iron, Cleek, Jigger, Mashie and Mashie-niblick, the modern equipment is identified by soulless numbers. This is also true of the modern golf ball and names like Silver King, Pin-hi, Tee-mee, Lynx, Bromford and Kro-flite are no longer with us.

From the first Open Championship at Prestwick in 1860 until the outbreak of the First World War British golfers dominated what was to become known as the greatest golfing accolade in Europe. In 1921 Jock Hutchinson, an expatriate Scot, won the title and in 1922 it was won by the first all-American player, Walter Hagen. Hagen won the title three more times after this, between one victory by Jim Barnes of the United States and the late Bobby Jones who won it in 1926 and 1927. After 1927 it was Hagen's turn again in 1928 and 1929. Bobby Jones recorded his third victory in 1930. Golfers from the United States of America continued to dominate the Open Championship until 1934 when Henry Cotton won. Cotton was followed by another home-bred player, Alfred Perry in 1935, A. H. Padgham in 1936 and Cotton's second win in 1937 was followed by two more British golfers in 1938 and 1939, R. A. Whitcombe and R. Burton respectively. There was no championship during the Second World War and the 1946 winner was yet another American, Samuel Jackson Snead. Apart from 1947 – Fred Daly – and 1948 when Henry Cotton recorded his third win, the Open Championship was dominated by overseas golfers until 1951 when it was won by Max Faulkner. A succession of visitors from abroad picked up the coveted title until another local lad in the shape of Tony Jacklin collected the famous urn in 1969.

By this time it was generally accepted that the golfing wheel had turned a full circle as far as design and equipment were concerned and that the balance of power was firmly in American hands as regarded technique. There were those who offered the obvious excuse, i.e. that there were more of 'them' than 'us' and it is true that by then there were certainly more golf courses in the United States. The Ryder Cup continued to be contested every two years as was the Walker Cup, but apart from a Ryder Cup win in 1957 in Lindrick and an equally unexpected win in the Walker Cup in 1971 at St Andrews we were no longer considered a power in world golf, either amateur or professional. This continued to be the case until a combined Great Britain and Europe side won the Ryder Cup at the Belfry in 1985, and when they retained it on American soil in 1987 they confirmed that the real power in world golf was now firmly vested in the golfers of Europe.

Many reasons have been offered as to why this is now so. We have always had golf courses that compare with the rest of the world, even if we have not always had the weather to complement them but with the development of golfing complexes in Europe, the increase in prize money and the use of the 1.68 golf ball, British and European golfers, amateur and professional, now believe in their ability to take on the best in the world and, as Tony Jacklin, our Ryder Cup Captain said after the 1987 victory, 'We are not frightened to go out and win.'

Almost all of the great championship courses in Great Britain and Ireland are true links courses, most of them helped along in the later stages by golf course designers and, in many instances, copied by other architects from other parts of the world. The leisure boom after the Second World War led to the construction of many fine golf courses in the resort areas of Spain and to a lesser extent in Portugal, together with new complexes in the south of France, but the earliest of the European courses was Pau which was built among the foothills of the Pyrenees in 1856.

In offering the reader a look at the golf courses of Europe I have selected what I consider to be the outstanding ones both in design and facilities. There is not sufficient room to mention every course and if I have missed one of your favourites then I trust that I have included one or two that you have not so far visited.

# What To Take and What To Leave Behind

## Passport and airline tickets

Do ensure that you have a visa if you need one. Your travel agent should be able to advise you.

## Holiday insurance

This can be obtained through most banks or through your travel agent and should cover sickness, loss and damage. There are policies which also cover flight delays, etc. If travelling by car a green card should be obtained from your car insurance company.

## Handicap certificate

Most golf clubs now require the sight of a valid handicap certificate.

## Baggage

Baggage allowance when travelling by air is 20 kg/44 lb and carriage of golf clubs is free with some airlines whilst others allow the first 4 kilos free of charge. Your golf clubs should be weighed separately from your other baggage, but do check with the individual carrier *before* commencing your journey. This will save a deal of aggravation at the check-in desk on departure.

## Golf bag and clubs

A lightweight golf bag with a hood will usually hold the full 14 clubs if you need them for your holiday golf but in most instances a half-set of say, a driver, 3, 5, 7, 9, 10 and a putter is adequate, especially if you intend to carry your golf clubs when playing. Small padlocks for the hood of the golf bag and for the golf ball pockets will act as a deterrent to light-fingered types.

## Coverall

A stout coverall can be bought from most golf equipment manufacturers and will help to protect your clubs in transit. The coverall

A roof rack is often the best place for carrying clubs and other equipment

will also help you to identify your equipment on the carousel at the end of a flight.

## Golf balls

Whilst the current price of golf balls is the same in the UK and Ireland, they are often more expensive in other countries so do take as many as you can comfortably carry in your golf bag. On many of the golf courses in Europe you may find itinerant sellers of golf balls who offer balls that they have 'found' on the various courses. Most golf clubs do not encourage this practice and, in any event, you will rarely get a 'bargain' price.

## Golf gloves

As with golf balls, the reputable makes are usually the same price in the UK and Ireland but in some countries – Spain for example – locally manufactured golf gloves are generally of reasonable quality and can be cheaper.

## Sun hats

Over-exposure of the head can spoil a golfing holiday from the first day in the warmer climates and a floppy sun hat is well worth a couple of pounds or so. The professional's shop at the golf club usually has a good supply but in most instances, the addition of the club logo on the hat can add a bit to the price. And whilst a hat may do nothing for your golf it could prevent sun-stroke!

## Golf shoes

Take your favourite pair of golf shoes with you; lightweight ones for hot climates which can be carried inside the golf bag whilst in transit. Rubber shoes are not advisable in warm climates as they make the feet very hot and uncomfortable. As with most golf equipment, shoes are very expensive in most European countries.

## Golf shirts and sweaters

Good quality brand names vary little in price in the UK and Ireland but in other countries, they can be prohibitive, as they are imported. Some countries in Europe do manufacture their own shirts but the quality can vary considerably. So it is best to take them with you.

## Golf trousers

The recognised makes of golf trousers can be just as expensive so a visit to your professional's shop before you leave for your holiday is advisable.

## Waterproof clothing and umbrellas

A set of waterproof clothing can be carried in the side pocket of your golf bag and an umbrella can be carried inside the golf bag with your clubs without adding too much weight. Only the most optimistic of golfers will travel without either and even the more temperate climes do have rain from time to time!

## Camera and film

There is nothing nicer than a photographic record of your holiday, wherever you may spend it, but *do* carry your camera with you and *don't* leave it lying around on the seat of your car when the vehicle is unattended, even if the car is locked. Put it out of sight, either in the boot or in the glove compartment.

If you are travelling by air do pass your camera and film *around* the X-ray security check at the airport. There are notices displayed at most checks which state that the equipment does not damage film but in my experience some equipment is inclined to 'fog' unexposed film or film that has not been processed. Do purchase all the film that you will require before going on holiday. If you are travelling by air, film is not cheaper in duty free shops and in some countries it can be quite expensive. Moreover you will often not find the particular brand or quality that you want.

## Money

When holidaying outside the United Kingdom it is advisable to carry your holiday money in travellers' cheques. There are ample bureaux de change in most countries, and the rates of exchange can be better than at the banks. But do check before you change your money into the local currency. If you are going to a bank outside the UK you will need to take your passport with you. Do not carry cash if you can possibly avoid it. Wallets should not be carried in back pockets, especially in crowded areas; nor should handbags be carried dangling by their shoulder straps. A small handbag or holdall that will hold most of your valuables is a sensible article and it will fit easily inside one of the pockets on your golf bag. Do not leave any valuable items in the golf club whilst you are out playing, expecting to find them still there when you return – it could ruin a good day's golf!

If you are enjoying the facilities of a villa for your holiday – especially in Spain – do be aware of gipsy-type women who try to sell you local products like table cloths etc. Whilst they are engaging your attention a confederate will be inside the villa stealing loose cash and other easily disposable items. This happens all too frequently, unfortunately, and I have had personal experience of such light-fingered visitors.

## Sun tan lotions and sun-glasses

Buy the sort of protective oil or cream that suits your skin. Your local chemist will advise you. Prices vary and, if you are flying, they are lower in the duty free shops although they may not have your particular choice. Do not try to get a tan on the first day of your holiday, wherever you may be, and if you are golfing in shorts do remember that exposed knees and legs can burn just as easily!

If you wear sun-glasses do remember to put some sort of protective covering on your nose. An hour in the sun with the rays reflected off the metal parts of the sun-glasses has ruined many a nose in a matter of minutes.

# Driving

Personally, the first thing I leave behind is my car, and there are a number of reasons why it can be better to take one of the various golfing package tours.

The most important consideration is that all the operators specialise in complete holidays for the golfer which include the best available accommodation, and the all-inclusive cost is much cheaper. In the package they offer preferred teeing-off times at a number of selected courses during the holiday whereas if you travel alone, it is more than likely that when you arrive at a golf course, all the starting times are booked for that week, and possibly the next week as well! Hire cars are usually included in the package deal and can be collected at the point of arrival with the minimum of fuss. The golfing package tour operators are also able to offer cheaper green fees at selected golf courses and, for the competitive golfer, a series of competitions during the stay. The various activities on offer are optional, of course, and do not preclude the golfer who wishes to do his own thing during the holiday.

The cost of the hire car can be included in your holiday and supplements are payable on sole occupancy and on larger cars. Regulations for driving a hire car vary from country to country. Your travel agent or tour operator will advise you. All hire cars on golfing package deals are fitted with roof-racks as standard and are also equipped with strong elastic straps to secure the luggage that may be carried on the roof-rack. It is standard practice with most hire cars that they have been checked and serviced before collection and that there is a full tank of petrol. Do check the fuel gauge before leaving the collection point as you will be expected to leave the car with the same amount of fuel in the tank at the end of your holiday or be charged for the difference. It is also advisable to check the vehicle for external damage before setting out and point out any old damage to the operator.

Documents appertaining to the hire vehicle are always carried on the car and this includes the insurance. Outside the UK hire cars are identified by a small windscreen ticket.

Do remember that in Europe vehicles coming from the right have priority and that it is much safer to make a right turn than a left!

If you are taking your own car, check the spare wheel before you travel. It is always advisable to carry a small emergency kit of fan belt, etc. that can be obtained from most auto factors. A good torch or a multi-purpose lantern and easy-to-read maps should travel in the car with you and last, but by no means least, carry a first aid kit.

# SCOTLAND

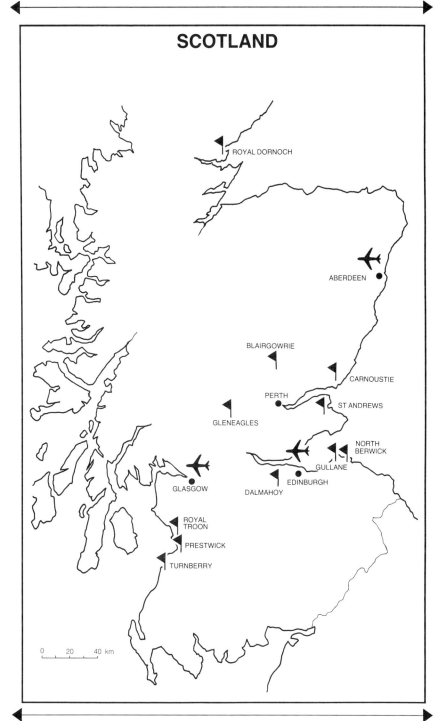

# SCOTLAND

ROYAL DORNOCH

ABERDEEN

BLAIRGOWRIE

CARNOUSTIE

PERTH

ST ANDREWS

GLENEAGLES

NORTH BERWICK

GULLANE

GLASGOW

DALMAHOY

EDINBURGH

ROYAL TROON

PRESTWICK

TURNBERRY

0   20   40 km

# Introduction

Golf as we know it today started in Scotland on wild, windswept areas of land that were fit, said a luxury-loving pal of mine, only 'for blasted sheep and the devil.' But despite this invective he joined the hundreds and thousands of golfers who, even if they were not in love with the wild and unforgiving landscape, as self-confessed golf nuts, just had to put it on record that they *had* played on the championship links that abound in the land of haggis and bagpipes.

And whilst no definite records exist as to when golf was first played in Scotland it was known to be a popular game in 1411 when the University of St Andrews was founded. The first official mention of the game was in laws passed by the Scottish Parliament from 1457 to 1491 which prohibited the game of golf as it had become so popular as to interfere with the practice of archery. Archery, they said, was essential to the defence of Scotland against the marauding English.

Reference is also made in the archives that when the Union of Scotland and England took place in 1603, officials of the Court of King James who accompanied him to London eagerly sought out a piece of land at Blackheath and laid out the first golf course in England. That this piece of ground was common land was in keeping with the concept of the Scottish linksland. There are many more references to the game of golf after this and numerous complaints make reference to 'disorders and entrenchments' and the 'digging of sandpits' and 'defacing of fields'. A book in the Manchester Reference Library that was published around 1862 quotes an extract from a letter of Queen Catherine to Cardinal Wolsey dated 13th August, 1513 which says: 'All his subjects be very glad, I thank God, to be busy with the golf for they take it for pastime, my heart is very glad to it...'

If, as my friend suggested, links golf is not everyone's cup of tea St Andrews is still the shrine to which the greatest and the humblest return to pay homage. Scotland's pride is the natural links where time and tide have played equal parts in the formation of golf courses that have no equal in the hearts of golfers everywhere.

It is not possible to cover every golf course in Scotland so I have selected those about which all golfers of whatever handicap would like to say, 'Yes, I have played there.'

# Selected Courses

## St Andrews

At first sight I was not impressed with the Old Course and although I had written many words about the players I had no great desire to play it. On my first visit the grey clouds hung over the forbidding outline of the Royal and Ancient Clubhouse and a sea *har* chilled the unprotected extremities. Approaching the area of the 1st tee which seemed to be surrounded by equally forbidding small grey hotels and shops I congratulated myself on the fact that I had left my golf clubs back in England in favour of a notebook. Old Tom Morris's shop, I thought, was pretty unremarkable as was another wee emporium devoted to the sale of tweeds and the like. What I could see of what one writer had described as the 'superb bay and acres of golden sand' looked like the sodden back of a stray dog and as I walked the links for the very first time with the ice-cold mist reaching out to envelop me in its grey, twisted fingers I was uncharitable enough to say to myself: 'Only the Jocks would want to play a civilised game in such a Godforsaken spot as this!'

As I lurched from one hole to the next and contemplated the enormous greens on the outward nine holes it occurred to me that if I kept walking I could be back in England in no time at all. I was unable to appreciate what had been described as the 'subtleties' of the Old Course and I had decided that the word 'brutal' would be a more apt expression.

On my first sight of the approach to the 17th green as I skirted the old railway sheds I decided that the masochistic challenge of hitting golf balls in this neck of the woods was definitely not for Mrs Humphreys' little lad! and I later described the problem of trying to hit the 17th green with any kind of second shot as rather like trying to hit a belly-dancer's 'G' string with a strand of wet spaghetti. But like a woman, the Old Course gets to you eventually, and not necessarily in the pocket, and, like a woman, it can be demanding, frustrating, unforgiving and unpredictable. It has attracted more golfers than any other course in the world and it will continue to do so for as long as golf is played.

The outline of the Old Course has not changed for over 400 years and is shaped like a shepherd's crook with the curve of the handle formed by holes 7, 8, 9, 10 and 11. There was not room for separate

The clubhouse of St Andrews

holes going out and coming home so the golfers played eleven holes out to the turn by the Eden estuary and then returned using the same fairways and greens, and seven of the double greens remain.

Most of the greens are on plateaux, some not much higher than the surrounding land but plateaux nevertheless. The turf, which was usually hard and not receptive to high pitched shots, has altered somewhat with the addition of automatic watering. The pitch and run shot is still required on the approach to many greens.

The bunkers are many and varied, ranging from huge sandy wastes to small, sharply contoured ones with barely enough room for a thin golfer and a 1 iron. All of these bunkers are natural, some made by man in his quest for shells, others by sheep seeking shelter. Many have been filled in over the years but the ones that remain are not always visible to the golfer.

**Location:** Nearest towns: Dundee, 13 miles; Perth, 32 miles; Edinburgh, 56 miles. Four public links: Old; New; Eden and Jubilee. All are located at St Andrews Links.
Further details can be obtained from: Links Management Committee, Golf Place, St Andrews, Fife, KY16 9JA.
**Telephone:** (0334) 5757.

**Information for Visitors:** Old Course: Reservations eight weeks in advance or by daily ballot April–October (contact starter, Tel: 3393). Closed Sundays, restricted July and August, preference to local players Thursdays and Saturdays. New Course: Reservations eight weeks in advance at additional fee. Eden: Reservations eight weeks in advance.

**Length:** Old Course: Out 3528 yards, In 3432 yards, Total 6960 yards. New Course: 6604 yards. Eden: 5971 yards. Jubilee: 6284 yards.

**Par:** Old Course: Out 39, In 36, Total 72. New Course: 70. Eden: 70. Jubliee: 69.

**Accommodation:** Old Course Hotel, Tel: (0334) 74371; Scores Hotel, Tel: 72451; Rusacks Hotel, Tel: 74321.

**Card of the Course:**

| No. | 1. | Burn | 370 yards par 4 |
| No. | 2. | Dyke | 411 yards par 4 |
| No. | 3. | Cartgate (out) | 398 yards par 4 |
| No. | 4. | Ginger Beer | 463 yards par 4 |
| No. | 5. | Hole o'Cross (out) | 564 yards par 5 |
| No. | 6. | Heathery (out) | 416 yards par 4 |
| No. | 7. | High (out) | 372 yards par 4 |
| No. | 8. | Short | 178 yards par 3 |
| No. | 9. | End | 356 yards par 4 |
| No. | 10. | Bobby Jones | 342 yards par 4 |
| No. | 11. | High (in) | 172 yards par 3 |
| No. | 12. | Heathery (in) | 316 yards par 4 |
| No. | 13. | Hole o' Cross (in) | 425 yards par 4 |
| No. | 14. | Long | 567 yards par 5 |
| No. | 15. | Cartgate (in) | 413 yards par 4 |
| No. | 16. | Corner of the Dyke | 382 yards par 4 |
| No. | 17. | Road | 461 yards par 4 |
| No. | 18. | Tom Morris | 354 yards par 4 |

# Carnoustie

Carnoustie is another of the great links courses and is possibly one of the toughest tests in golf. It was a long golf course by any standards when it was first opened in 1842 and when it was extended for the 1968 Open it measured some 7100 yards. It lies on the flatlands between the Tay estuary and the distant small hills and is subject to the constantly changing winds. Like many other links layouts a hole that on one day is only a drive and a pitch becomes a physical challenge with every club in the bag, even from the medal tees, when the wind blows from the opposite direction.

The ten-hole course that was laid out by Allan Robertson was long enough but even after the extension to eighteen holes under the guidance of Tom Morris it was subjected to further changes until James Braid was invited to design new tees, greens and bunkers in 1926. The result was a superb course that was to test the greatest golfers in the world and of some 300 young men from the area who turned professional a great number went to the United States to seek their fame and fortune. It has been said that the development of American golf owes much of its strength to these young men of Carnoustie and it is a fact that any number of of its features have been incorporated in other courses throughout the world.

Within the confines of Carnoustie is another, smaller eighteen-hole course called the Burnside and both courses, together with the four clubs that share them, are held in trust by the town council. This council provides a joint management committee.

Flatter than most British championship links it is made more difficult by the two burns which meander through the course. Jockie's Burn comes into play at the 2nd, 3rd, 5th and 6th whilst the Barry Burn meanders through the fairways and is a particular hazard on the last two holes.

**Location:** Links Parade, Carnoustie, Angus, Tayside.
Nearest town: Dundee, 12 miles.
**Telephone:** (0241) 53249.
**Information for Visitors:** Visitors welcome on the Medal Course, weekdays, Burnside Course, weekends. A telephone call is advisable
**Length:** Medal Course: 6809 yards. Burnside Course: 5935 yards.
**Par:** Medal Course: 72. Burnside Course: 68.
**Accommodation:** Bruce Hotel, Links Parade, Tel: (0241) 52364.

**Card of the course:**

| No. | 1. Cup | 406 yards par 4 |
| No. | 2. Gulley | 464 yards par 4 |
| No. | 3. Jockie's Burn | 363 yards par 4 |
| No. | 4. Hillocks | 379 yards par 4 |

| No. | 5. | Brae | 397 yards par 4 |
| No. | 6. | Long | 524 yards par 5 |
| No. | 7. | Plantation | 397 yards par 4 |
| No. | 8. | Short | 174 yards par 3 |
| No. | 9. | Railway | 421 yards par 4 |
| No. | 10. | South America | 453 yards par 4 |
| No. | 11. | Dyke | 372 yards par 4 |
| No. | 12. | Southward Ho! | 478 yards par 5 |
| No. | 13. | Whins | 166 yards par 3 |
| No. | 14. | Spectacles | 488 yards par 5 |
| No. | 15. | Luckyslap | 461 yards par 4 |
| No. | 16. | Barry Burn | 235 yards par 3 |
| No. | 17. | Island | 454 yards par 4 |
| No. | 18. | Home | 448 yards par 4 |

# Turnberry

Turnberry, Ayrshire has two fine links courses which were founded in 1903. During the Second World War runways were built across both courses and Turnberry was an RAF training school for Spitfire pilots. It was reconstructed after the war and the Ailsa and Arran courses are now popular holiday golfing territory. Turnberry finally reached the status that many thought was overdue when it was selected as the venue for the 1977 Open Championship.

The Ailsa course is named after the huge Ailsa Craig rock which juts out of the waters of the Firth of Clyde whilst the other course, the Arran, gets its name from the Isle of Arran which is some 20 miles away. Ailsa is the championship course but Arran is an equally good test of golf.

The complex was the creation of the London, Midland and Scottish Railway Company that flourished before the First World War and Turnberry was well established as a championship venue before the Second World War. There used to be a private rail link between the Turnberry Hotel which overlooks the two golf courses and the nearby town of Girvan but this was eventually scrapped as the motor car became more popular. The lovely hotel and its facilities have recently been upgraded and it still attracts thousands of golfers from all over the world.

Whilst the Ailsa course is a formidable test for the holiday golfer from the championship tees, the medal tees shorten the course by some 600 yards. There are many spectacular holes on the Ailsa course but none more photographed and talked about than the 9th. The championship tee literally rises out of the Atlantic with a sheer drop on three sides of the tiny teeing area and is not the most comforting spot to be standing when the wind is gusting as it often does.

The Ailsa is possibly my favourite links course in Europe but on either of the two courses in this lovely part of Scotland if you play to your handicap then you can feel justifiably pleased.

**Location:** Turnberry Hotel, Turnberry, Ayrshire.
**Telephone:** (065 53) 202.
**Information for Visitors:** Visitors are welcome by prior arrangement with the hotel and priority is given to hotel residents.
**Length:** Ailsa: Championship tees, 6936 yards; Medal tees, 6384 yards. Arran: 6350 yards.
**Par:** Ailsa: Championship tees, 73; Medal tees, 71. Arran: 70.
**Accommodation:** Turnberry Hotel (see above).

The lovely hotel which overlooks both courses at Turnberry

# Around Edinburgh

## Royal Burgess

**Location:** Whitehouse Rd, Barnton, Edinburgh.
Six miles from Edinburgh on A90 towards Forth Bridge.
**Telephone:** (031) 336 2075.
**Information for Visitors:** Visitors welcome. No ladies at weekends.
**Length:** 6604 yards.
**SSS:** 72.
**Accommodation:** Barnton Hotel, Queensferry Rd,
Tel: (031) 336 2291.

## Bruntisfield Links

**Location:** Barnton Avenue, Edinburgh.
Off A90 in Davidsons Mains.
**Telephone:** (031) 336 2006.
**Information for Visitors:** Visitors welcome.
**Length:** 6369 yards.
**SSS:** 70.
**Accommodation:** Barton Hotel, Queensferry Rd,
Tel: (031) 336 2291.

## Murrayfield

**Location:** Murrayfield Rd, Edinburgh.
Two miles west of city centre on A8.
**Telephone:** (031) 337 1009.
**Information for Visitors:** Visitors welcome Mondays to Fridays.
**Length:** 5724 yards.
**SSS:** 68.
**Accommodation:** Post House, Corstorphine Rd,
Tel: (031) 334 8221.

## Ratho Park

**Location:** Ratho. West of Edinburgh on A8 then left at B7030.
**Telephone:** (031) 333 1752.
**Information for Visitors:** Visitors welcome.
**Length:** 6020 yards.
**SSS:** 69.

**Accommodation:** Royal Scot Hotel, 111 Glasgow Rd, Edinburgh, Tel: (031) 334 9191.

# Duddingston

**Location:** Duddingston Rd West, Edinburgh.
South of Edinburgh off A1.
**Telephone:** (031) 661 7688.
**Information for Visitors:** Visitors welcome.
**Length:** 6647 yards.
**SSS:** 72.
**Accommodation:** Oratava Hotel, 41 Craigmillar Park, Edinburgh, Tel: (031) 667 9484.

# Royal Musselburgh

**Location:** Prestongrange House, Prestonpans.
North Berwick road from Wallyford roundabout on A1.
**Telephone:** (0875) 810276.
**Information for Visitors:** Visitors welcome.
**Length:** 6284 yards.
**SSS:** 70.
**Accommodation:** Sands Hotel, 55-56 Promenade, Portobello, Tel: (031) 669 8969.

# Dalmahoy

**Location:** Kirknewton, Midlothian.
Seven miles west of Edinburgh on A71.
**Telephone:** (031) 333 1275.
**Information for Visitors:** Visitors welcome.
**Length:** 6639 yards.
**SSS:** 67.
**Accommodation:** Norton House Hotel, Kirknewton, Tel: (031) 333 1845.

# Kingsknowe

**Location:** 326 Lanark Rd, Edinburgh. West of Edinburgh on A71.
**Telephone:** (031) 441 1145.
**Information for Visitors:** Visitors welcome, restricted at weekends.
**Length:** 5825 yards.
**SSS:** 68.

**Accommodation:** Hailes Hotel, 2 Wester Hailes Centre, Edinburgh, Tel: (031) 443 8082.

## Braid Hills

**Location:** Braid Hills, Lothian. Municipal course, heathland.
**Telephone:** (031) 447 6666.
**Information for Visitors:** Open to the public except Sundays.
**Length:** 5731 yards.
**SSS:** 68.
**Accommodation:** Braid Hills Hotel, Braid Rd, Braid Hills, Tel: (031) 447 8888.

## Torphin Hills

**Location:** Torphin Rd, Edinburgh.
**Telephone:** (031) 441 1100.
**Information for Visitors:** Visitors welcome.
**Length:** 5020 yards.
**SSS:** 66.
**Accommodation:** Braid Hills Hotel, Braid Rd, Braid Hills, Tel: (031) 447 8888.

## Broomieknowe

**Location:** Golf Course Rd, Bonnyrigg.
Seven miles south-east of Edinburgh.
**Telephone:** (031) 663 9317.
**Information for Visitors:** Visitors welcome.
**Length:** 6046 yards.
**SSS:** 69.
**Accommodation:** Oratava Hotel, 41 Craigmillar Park, Edinburgh, Tel: (031) 667 9484.

## Longniddry

**Location:** Longniddry, East Lothian. Thirteen miles east of Edinburgh. North Berwick road from Wallyford roundabout on A1.
**Telephone:** (0875) 52141.
**Information for Visitors:** Visitors welcome. Jacket and tie compulsory in dining room.
**Length:** 6240 yards.
**SSS:** 70.

**Accommodation:** Kilspindie House Hotel, Main St, Aberlady, Tel: (087 57) 319.

## Honourable Company of Edinburgh Golfers

**Location:** Muirfield, Gullane, East Lothian.
Twenty miles east of Edinburgh on A198.
**Telephone:** (0620) 842123.
**Information for Visitors:** Visitors welcome. Telephone first. Introductory letter from your own club secretary required. Ladies only with members.
**Length:** 6926 yards.
**SSS:** 73.
**Accommodation:** Marine Hotel, North Berwick, Tel: (0620) 2406.

## Gullane

**Location:** Gullane, East Lothian.
A1 from Edinburgh to Musselburgh then left on A198 to Gullane. Three courses and a 5-hole children's course.
**Telephone:** (0620) 843115.
**Information for Visitors:** Visitors welcome on courses 2 and 3 without a member.
**Length:** No 1: 6444 yards; No 2: 6090 yards; No 3: 5012 yards.
**SSS:** No 1: 71; No 2: 69; No 3: 64.
**Accommodation:** Greywalls Hotel, Duncur Rd, Gullane, Tel: (0620) 842144.

# Around Glasgow

## East Kilbride

**Location:** Nerston, East Kilbride.
Ten miles south of Glasgow on the A276.
**Telephone:** (035 52) 20913.
**Information for Visitors:** Visitors welcome only with member.
**Length:** 18 holes, 6484 yards.
**SSS:** 71.
**Accommodation:** Bruce Hotel, Cornwall St, Tel: (035 52) 29771.

# Cawder

**Location:** Cadder Estate, Bishopbriggs, Glasgow. To the north of Glasgow on the A803. Two courses, the Cawder and the Keir.
**Telephone:** (041) 772 7360.
**Information for Visitors:** Visitors welcome only with member.
**Length:** Cawder: 18 holes, 6307 yards. Keir: 18 holes, 5885 yards.
**SSS:** Cawder: 71. Keir: 68.
**Accommodation:** Black Bull Hotel, Main St, Milngavie,
Tel: (041) 956 2291.

# Whitecraigs

**Location:** Ayr Rd, Giffnock, Renfrewshire.
Seven miles south of Glasgow on the A77. Parkland course.
**Telephone:** (041) 839 4530.
**Information for Visitors:** Visitors welcome only with member.
**Length:** 18 holes, 6100 yards.
**SSS:** 68.
**Accommodation:** Macdonald Hotel, Eastwood Toll, Giffnock,
Tel: (041) 638 2225.

# Pollok

**Location:** 90 Barrhead Rd, Glasgow.
Four miles south-west of Glasgow on the A736. Parkland course.
**Telephone:** (041) 632 1080.
**Information for Visitors:** Visitors welcome with member, or on production of a letter from your own club secretary. Telephone first.
**Length:** 18 holes, 6257 yards.
**SSS:** 70.
**Accommodation:** Tinto Firs Hotel, 470 Kilmarnock Rd,
Tel: (041) 637 2353.

# Buchanan Castle

**Location:** Drymen, Glasgow. Seventeen miles north-west of Glasgow off the A809. Parkland course.
**Telephone:** (0360) 369.
**Information for Visitors:** Visitors welcome with member or on production of a letter from your own club secretary. Telephone first.
**Length:** 18 holes, 6032 yards.

**SSS:** 69.
**Accommodation:** Buchanan Arms Hotel, Tel: (0360) 588.

# Ranfurly Old Course

**Location:** Bridge of Weir, Renfrewshire.
West of Glasgow Airport off the A761.
**Telephone:** (0505) 612099.
**Information for Visitors:** Visitors welcome with member, or on production of a letter from your own club secretary. Telephone first.
**Length:** 18 holes, 6266 yards.
**SSS:** 70.
**Accommodation:** Excelsior Hotel, Abbotsinch, Renfrewshire, Tel: (041) 887 1212.

# Haggs Castle

**Location:** Dumbreck Rd, Glasgow.
South-west of Glasgow, near Ibrox Stadium.
**Telephone:** (041) 427 0480.
**Information for Visitors:** Visitors welcome only with member.
**Length:** 18 holes, 6464 yards.
**SSS:** 71.
**Accommodation:** Sherbrooke Hotel, 11 Sherbrooke Ave., Pollokshields, Tel: (041) 427 4277.

# Milngavie

**Location:** Laigh Park, Milngavie, Glasgow.
North-west of Glasgow on the A809.
**Telephone:** (041) 956 1619.
**Information for Visitors:** Visitors welcome only with member.
**Length:** 5818 yards.
**SSS:** 68.
**Accommodation:** Black Bull Hotel, Main St, Milngavie, Tel: (041) 956 2291.

# Other Places to Play

**North Berwick.** Beach Rd, North Berwick, East Lothian.
Tel: (0620) 2135.
**Gleneagles.** Gleneagles Hotel, Perthshire. Tel: (076 46) 2231. The
hotel is closed from October to Easter, so this is often the best time
to play.
**Rosemount.** Blairgowrie. Tel: (0250) 2622. One of the loveliest
courses in Europe.
**Lundin Links.** Golf Rd, Lundin Links. Tel: (0333) 320202.
**Ladybank.** Annsmuir, Ladybank. Tel: (0337) 30320.
**Nairn.** Seabank Rd, Nairn. Tel: (0667) 52103.
**Elgin.** Hardhillock Birnie Rd, Elgin. Tel: (0343) 2338.
**Royal Dornoch.** Golf Rd, Dornock. Tel: (0862) 810219.
**Royal Troon.** Craigend Rd, Troon. Tel: (0292) 311555.
**Pres⁺wick.** Links Rd, Prestwick. Tel: (0292) 77404.
**Barassie.** Hillhouse Rd, Barassie, Troon. Tel: (0292) 311077.
**Gailes.** Gailes Irvine, Ayrshire. Tel: (0294) 311649.

The Gleneagles Hotel, Perthshire

# IRELAND

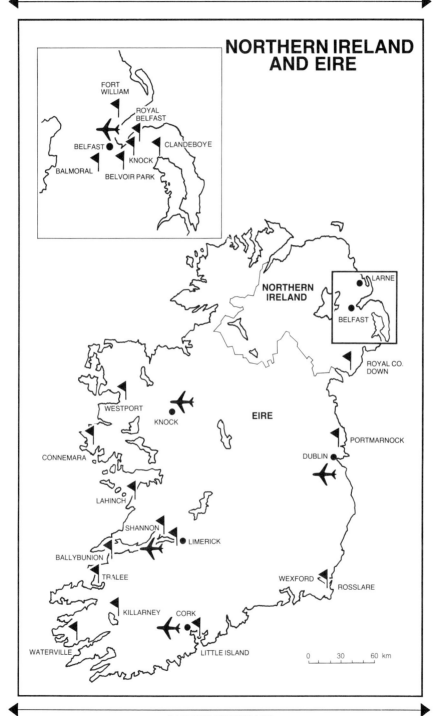

# NORTHERN IRELAND AND EIRE

FORT WILLIAM

ROYAL BELFAST

BELFAST

CLANDEBOYE

KNOCK

BALMORAL

BELVOIR PARK

NORTHERN IRELAND

LARNE

BELFAST

ROYAL CO. DOWN

WESTPORT

KNOCK

EIRE

PORTMARNOCK

CONNEMARA

DUBLIN

LAHINCH

SHANNON

LIMERICK

BALLYBUNION

TRALEE

WEXFORD

ROSSLARE

KILLARNEY

CORK

WATERVILLE

LITTLE ISLAND

0     30     60 km

# Introduction

An old friend of mine who is a devotee of golf in Ireland once said to me: 'One of the nice things about Ireland is that if you just turn up at a golf club there is always someone waiting to give you a game. They always apologise after they have beaten you and leave you in no doubt that they don't usually play as well. Also, drinks appear on the bar like shafts of sunlight through a virgin's hair and they never say, "Would you like another", but, "those three are yours" *and*, they *never* discuss the game that you have just played.'

Getting to Ireland is fairly simple by boat and train and there are regular shuttle flights from Heathrow, Birmingham and Manchester to Belfast. There are regular flights also to Dublin, Cork and Shannon, and car ferries operate from several ports. Once there, there are glorious, uncrowded courses, green fees that must be the cheapest in Europe, first-class accommodation, good food, and a warm welcome from all and sundry. What more could a holiday golfer want except perfect weather. And if that is not always to hand it does not detract from the delights of Royal Portrush, Royal County Down, Portmarnock and Killarney. These are courses that most golfers will be familiar with but some of the lesser known ones south are real gems in their own right.

It was my old friend, Henry Longhurst who, when writing of golf in the south-west of Ireland said, 'Some of the Irish links, I was about to write, stand in comparison with the greatest in the world. They don't, they *are* the greatest in the world.' And of Killarney he said, 'What a lovely place to die.' But whether the individual choice is North or South, for scenic beauty, peace and idyllic playing conditions I know of no better place than the Emerald Isle.

# Northern Ireland

## Introduction

Using Belfast as a starting point for your golfing holiday there are any number of hotels and guest houses and a number of them have a special deal for golfers. A list is always available from the Northern Ireland Tourist Board and as all restaurants, eating houses, hotels and guest houses are carefully vetted and controlled by the Tourist Board, visiting golfers can book anywhere and be assured of the very best and at very reasonable prices.

## Selected Courses – Belfast Area

### Clandeboye

Clandeboye has two beautifully situated golf courses, the Ava and the Dufferin part on old heathland and part on parkland with gorse bushes being the dominating feature. There are some striking views over Strangford Lough and out towards the Isle of Man and the well-appointed clubhouse offers good food and warm hospitality. It is a good starting point for a golfing holiday in the North.

**Location:** Newtonards, Co. Down.
Between Belfast and Bangor.
**Telephone:** (0247) 465767.
**Length:** First course: 5172 metres. Second course: 6072 metres.
**SSS:** First course: 67. Second course: 73.
**Accommodation:** It is not far from the Culloden Hotel, Craigarad and the Royal Bangor Hotel.

### Belvoir Park

This course is laid out on rolling parkland. It was designed by Harry Colt, the man who designed Sunningdale and other well known courses.

**Location:** Church Rd, Newtonbreda, Belfast. About three miles south of Belfast.

**Telephone:** (0232) 641159.
**Information for Visitors:** Visitors are welcome at nearly all times. A telephone call will normally suffice.
**Length:** 6276 yards.
**SSS:** 71.

# Balmoral

This is a flat, parkland course and although a relatively short course, it is a good test of golf.

**Location:** On the Lisburn road, close to Belfast.
**Telephone:** (0232) 668540.
**Information for Visitors:** Visitors are welcome by prior arrangement.
**Length:** 6197 yards.
**SSS.** 70.

# Royal Belfast

The Royal Belfast is the oldest golf club in Ireland and celebrated its centenary in 1981. It is a real beauty of a course and is possibly the best in the Belfast area although there may well be other stalwarts who will tell you otherwise! It is a 'must' on any golfer's travels in this area.

**Location:** Craigavad, six miles from Belfast on the Bangor road.
**Telephone:** (023 17) 2368.
**Information for Visitors:** Telephone first. A letter from your own club secretary is necessary.
**Length:** 6205 yards.
**SSS:** 70.

# Fortwilliam

Also in the Belfast area this is a short course by most standards. It is a hilly, parkland course.

**Location:** Three miles north of Belfast.
**Telephone:** (0232) 771770.
**Information for Visitors:** Visitors welcome.
**Length:** 5275 yards.
**SSS:** 67.

## Knock

Set in parkland, this course has no rough to speak of (good for holiday golfers!) but it does have around 78 bunkers to compensate for the lack of rough.

**Location:** Five miles east of Belfast.
**Telephone:** (023 18) 2249.
**Length:** 5845 metres.
**SSS:** 71.

## Royal County Down

The Royal County Down is most certainly one of the four best courses anywhere in the British Isles. It is a links course at its best, on a windy coast it plays every inch and has huge sand dunes to delight or frustrate the golfer. The green fees, in keeping with the rest of Ireland, verge on the ridiculous! The Mountains of Mourne really do 'sweep down to the sea'.

**Location:** Thirty miles south of Belfast.
**Telephone:** (039 67) 2209.
**Information for Visitors:** A letter of introduction is required, and Wednesdays and Sundays are best avoided.

The Mountains of Mourne provide a marvellous backdrop to the Royal County Down course

**Length:** 6651 yards.
**Accommodation:** The Slieve Donard Hotel (Tel: (039 67) 23681)
adjoins the course and is on the edge of the sea. There are many
other delightful small hotels in the area.

# Other Places To Play

**Bainbridge**, Co. Down. Huntly Rd, Bainbridge Tel: (082) 06 22342.
**Ballycastle**, Co. Antrim. Cushendall Rd, Ballycastle.
Tel: (026) 57 62536.
**Ballyclare**, Co. Antrim. Springvale Rd, Ballyclare.
Tel: (096) 03 22857.
**Ballymena**, Co. Antrim. Raceview Rd, Ballymena.
Tel: (0266) 861487.
**Bangor**, Co. Down. Broadway, Bangor. Tel: (0247) 473922.
**Bushfoot**, Co. Antrim. Portballintrae. Tel: (026) 57 31317.
**Cairndhu**, Co. Antrim. Ballygally, Larne. Tel: (0574) 83324.

The Ballycastle course on the coast of County Antrim

**Carnalea**, Co. Down. Station Rd, Bangor. Tel: (0247) 461368.
**Carrickfergus**, Co. Antrim. North Rd, Carrickfergus.
Tel: (096) 03 62203.
**Castlerock**, Co. Londonderry. Tel: (0265) 848314.
**City Of Derry**, Co. Londonderry. Tel: (0504) 46369.
**Cliftonville**, Belfast. Westland Rd, Belfast. Tel: (0232) 744158.
**County Armagh**, Co. Armagh. Newry Rd, Armagh.
Tel: (0861) 522501.
**Cushendall**, Co. Antrim. Ballymena. Tel: (026) 67 71318.
**Donaghadee**, Co. Down. Warren Rd, Donaghadee.
Tel: (0247) 883624.
**Downpatrick**, Co. Down. Saul Rd, Downpatrick. Tel: (0396) 2152.
**Dungannon**, Co. Tyrone. Tel: (086) 22098.
**Dunmurry**, Belfast. Dunmurry Lane, Belfast. Tel: (0232) 610834.
**Enniskillen**, Co. Fermanagh. Tel: (0365) 25250.
**Greenisand**, Co. Antrim. Carrickfergus. Tel: (0231) 62236.
**Helen's Bay** , Co. Down. Bangor. Tel: (0247) 852601.
**Holywood**, Co. Down. Demense Rd, Holywood. Tel: (023) 17 3135.
**Kilkeel**, Co. Down. Ballayardle, Newry. Tel: (069) 37 62296.
**Kilrea**, Co. Londonderry. Coleraine. Tel: (026) 653 397.
**Larne**, Co. Antrim. Islandmagee, Larne. Tel: (096) 03 82228.
**Lisburn**, Co. Antrim. Eglantine Rd, Lisburn. Tel: (084) 77216.
**Lurgan**, Co. Armagh. Windsor Ave, Lurgan. Tel: (076) 22 22087.
**Mahee Island**, Co. Down. Newtownards. Tel: (0238) 541234.
**Malone**, Belfast. Malone Rd, Dunmurry, Belfast.
Tel: (0232) 612758.
**Newtownstewart**, Co. Tyrone. Tel: (066) 26 61466.
**Omagh**, Co. Tyrone. Dublin Rd, Omagh. Tel: (0662) 3160.
**Portadown**, Co. Armagh. Gilford Rd, Portadown.
Tel: (0762) 335356.
**Scrabo**, Co. Down. Newtownards. Tel: (0247) 812355.
**Shandon Park**, Belfast. Tel: (0232) 794856.
**Warrenpoint**, Co. Down. Tel: (096) 73695.
**Whitehead**, Co. Antrim. Carrickfergus. Tel: (096) 03 78631.

# Eire

## Introduction

The variety and quality of the golf courses in Eire provides a constant talking point as to which is the greatest, best, most scenic and I doubt if there will ever be total agreement. There are golfers who prefer the open, windswept challenge of courses like Ballybunion and Rosses Point on the shores of the Atlantic whilst the more somnambulistic will always opt for the dream-like quality of the lakeside, mountain-clad backdrop of Killarney. The more aggressive golfer obviously prefers the changing mood of Portmarnock but even here, in the height of summer, with a gentle breeze stirring the grasses, you can find a veritable sheep in wolf's clothing.

## Selected Courses

### Ballybunion

When a golfer of the calibre of Tom Watson says that Ballybunion is the 'best in the world' and the American golf writer, Herbert Warren Wynd adds that 'it is the finest sea-side course that I have ever seen', any other comment seems superfluous. Golf writer Peter Dobereiner is on record as saying that, in his opinion, the course was a masterpiece and golf architect, Robert Trent Jones reckons that the string of par fives on the New Course may come to be regarded as the greatest to be played on any course in the world.

Ballybunion is about an hour and a half by road from Cork along narrow, winding country roads with a general lack of traffic. One is liable to meet a number of agricultural vehicles en route and the odd collection of farm animals but this, to me, adds to the rural charm. My companion on one such trip, a dour Yorkshireman, swore that the road signs were all calculated to confuse but when it was pointed out to him that the Irish road signs are in two units – white means miles and green means kilometres – and that we were not further away than when we started, his degree in engineering came to the fore.

He did say afterwards that in his view, both Ballybunion courses were absolutely brilliant and he reminded me of Tom Watson's

Ballybunion, regarded by some as the best course in the world

statement that all budding golf course architects should visit and play there before even thinking of course design. Robert Trent Jones, the doyen of golf course designers, added that he thought that it was 'the finest piece of linksland' that he had ever seen, but as my Yorkie pal said: 'I don't suppose he took any notice of Watson.'

Ballybunion Old Course began its life in the last century as a 'short' course and was extended to 18 holes in 1926. The architect who was called in to effect the necessary alterations to the course before the 1937 Irish Amateur decided that the only contribution he could make was to add one fairway bunker and to move three greens. It was not possible, he said, to improve on perfection. One of the many superlatives that have been used to describe Ballybunion was that the links course was a masterpiece and probably the greatest links course in the world. For my part I am prepared to say that both courses provide some jolly fine golf in extremes of Atlantic wind and rain.

On our first day the wind was strong enough to make the sea-birds fly backwards and the umbrella was about as useful as a third arm to a one-legged tinker. A booklet issued by the Irish Tourist Board says: 'There is not much climate in Kerry...' There is, however, 'a great deal of weather, strong winds from the Atlantic and much rain'. Which is all quite true but little comfort to the fine weather golfer. Some 12 hours later, with the soft still air and an occasional zephyr breeze, even my companion, who was born and bred to the hard weather of his native Yorkshire, was heard to remark that it was a 'grand place to play golf'. Some hours earlier his comments would not have been printable. But despite its weather, Ballybunion is a bit special.

**Location:** 1³/₄ hours drive from Cork or Shannon airport.
**Telephone:** (068) 27146.
**Length:** Old Course: 6542 yards. New Course: 6477 yards.
**SSS:** 71

## Tralee

About 50 minutes' drive south from Ballybunion is the hamlet of Barrow, and close to, on a narrow, wristy piece of land that juts out into the Atlantic ocean is Tralee Golf Club. 'We used to have a lousy little nine-holer' said one of the golfing locals 'and in winter it was fit only for losing your mother-in-law.' So it was sold to a developer and with the cash from this transaction, in 1981 the present course was built. Opened for play in 1984 there are still facets to be incorporated.

The golf course lies on the cliffs and across the estuary one can see the Dingle Peninsula. My informant was quick to tell me that the cliffs were used in the film, *Ryan's Daughter* and the huge expanse of golden sand was 'the finest in all the world', but even making due allowance for Irish hyperbole it was difficult not to make comparisons between Tralee and the Monterey Peninsula of California.

**Location:** West Barrow, Ardfert, Co. Kerry.
**Telephone:** (066) 51150.
**Length:** 6210 metres.
**SSS:** 72.

The beautiful, landscaped course at Killarney, lying in the shadow of Macgillycuddy's Reeks

## Killarney

Turn inland from Tralee, travel south and the extremes of weather are quickly forgotten on the classic parkland courses of Killarney.

The spacious wooded grounds for the Killarney Golf and Fishing Club were provided by Lord Castlerosse. Sited on the shores of the lakes that were made famous in a song by Bing Crosby the 36-hole golf complex lies in the shadows of Macgillycuddy's Reeks. The first of these two courses, Mahony's Point, does not quite come in the same category as Muirfield and Birkdale, but the matchless setting places it in a category of its own.

When the stretch of trees and scrubland situated on sandy soil and bordering Lough Leane was suggested as the possible site for a new golf course the club committee, which had previously played golf over the Old Deer Park for a token rent of one shilling a year, was horrified when it was proposed by the estate's agent that the club rent should be increased to £75. After a hurried meeting they asked if they could take over this area, and it was at this point that

Lord Castlerosse, a scratch golfer in his early days, took a personal interest in the new proposals and saw the chance of creating a golf course that would surpass anything that the original parkland course had to offer. Sir Guy Campbell was engaged to design the new course and Lord Castlerosse invited Henry Longhurst, a close personal friend, to add his thoughts to the layout.

The opening of the new course in 1939 was overshadowed by the outbreak of the Second World War and since then many changes have taken place. New trees were planted and several tees were repositioned, and it has been said that of all the alterations it is the 193-yard, par 3, 13th hole that bears the unmistakable stamp of the golfing lord. It is possibly the most difficult of all the 36 holes.

The completion of the second 18 holes at Killarney finalised the creation of two completely new courses on which the old and the new holes are stylishly intermingled. The championship layout is made up from both courses – Mahony's Point and Killeen – and the famous lake comes into play on twelve holes.

Inspired by the intrinsic beauty of Augusta National, USA, Castlerosse had intended to plant every part of the course with multi-coloured trees and shrubs such as he had seen at Augusta but his work was unfinished at the time of his death in 1943. A giant of a man with the enthusiasm and personality to match, he has left much of his style and stamp on Killarney and I feel sure that he would heartily approve.

And if the par 3, 202-yard, 18th hole at Mahony's Point has been described by some purists as an 'unconventional' ending it is a fact that the two courses are amongst the most breathtakingly beautiful in the world.

**Location:** Mahony's Point, Killarney.
**Telephone:** (064) 31034.
**Length:** Mahony's Point: 6758 yards. Killeen: 6798 yards.
**SSS:** Mahony's Point: 70. Killeen: 72.

# Waterville

Waterville is about a two-hour run from Killarney and sits on the Ring of Kerry tourist route.

Irish-American Jack Mulcahy was the designer of what has since been described by the legendary Sam Snead as 'the beautiful monster' which was opened for play in 1974. Sandwiched between the mountains and the Ballinskelligs Bay it has long been a tourist attraction and among the more notable of its visitors have been

Charlie Chaplin, Bob Hope, Sam Snead, Doug Sanders, Tom Watson and Sean Connery. It ranks as one of the longest courses in Europe and if the first nine holes are fairly routine the homeward nine are a different ball game.

It may well be that Mulcahy sought to lull the unsuspecting golfer into a false sense of reasonable security but before you start thinking that perhaps this is not your cup of tea be reassured by the comments of Liam Higgins, the resident professional and himself no mean hitter of the ball, who said that the course has equal merits off the forward tees. Quite what he meant by that is anyone's guess but Waterville is complemented by the attendant facilities and has been described as a gourmet's haven.

Like a number of golf courses throughout the world it has one hole that sticks in the memory long after the holiday is over. The view from Mulcahy's Peak, the 17th tee, is one that all will remember even if they do not hit the nearby green, and it is most definitely calculated to act as a soother before tackling the monstrous 18th hole. It is, as American Claud Harmon said, 'One of the golfing wonders of the world'.

**Location:** Waterville Lake Hotel.
**Telephone:** (0667) 4102.
**Length:** 7146 yards.
**SSS:** 74.

## Lahinch

It was the Scots who introduced golf to Lahinch in 1893 but it was not until 1928 that Dr Alister Mackenzie – the architect of Augusta National – was asked to put his ideas to work and when he had finished he said: 'It will make the finest and most popular course that I have constructed.' Whether or not that was an overstatement matters not, it does give some indication of the stature of Lahinch – known as the Irish St Andrews – as a fine links course, even if the redoubtable doctor was not allowed to touch the long 5th and the short 6th. This to my mind was a great pity as the latter hole, a par 3, is blind and does little for the peace of mind of us holiday hackers. There is also a short holiday course which runs around the lone tower of O'Brien's Castle and is a most pleasant 18 holes.

**Location:** About 30 miles north-west of Shannon Airport.
**Telephone:** (065) 81003.

'The Irish St Andrews' – Lahinch golf course, County Clare

**Length:** Championship Course: 6515 yards.
No. 2 Course: 5450 yards.
**SSS:** Championship Course: 72. No. 2 Course: 67.

## Shannon

Lying close to the River Shannon's estuary this course was designed by the late John Harris. Its major problem is its proximity to the river and it does suffer in the aftermath of prolonged wet weather.

**Location:** Shannon Airport.
**Telephone:** (061) 61849.
**Length:** 6900 yards.
**SSS:** 73.

## Cork

East of Kerry lies the largest county in the whole of Ireland, Co. Cork. The county boasts no less than 19 courses and foremost amongst these is Cork Golf Club, another course that had the attentions of Dr Alister Mackenzie. Overlooking the town's harbour on Little Island one of its more famous son's was Jimmy Bruen of Walker Cup fame. Bruen was a member of the victorious team that beat the Americans in 1938, was equally well known in golfing circles for the 'loop' in his swing and was the British Amateur Champion in 1946.

**Location:** Little Island, Co. Cork.
**Telephone:** (021) 353451.
**Length:** 6065 metres.
**SSS:** 72.

## Limerick

Limerick Golf Club was founded in 1891 by golfing officers of the Black Watch Regiment of Scotland. It was these officers who also turned their minds and talents for golf course building to Lahinch.

**Location:** Three miles from Limerick.
**Telephone:** (061) 44083.
**Length:** 5767 yards.
**SSS:** 70.

# Other Places To Play

## Dublin and the east

**Arklow**, Co. Wicklow. Tel: (0402) 32492.
**Balbriggan**, Co. Dublin. Tel: 01 412173.
**Beaverstown**, Co. Dublin. Tel: 01 452721.
**Bodenstown**, Co. Kildare. Tel. (045) 97096.
**Castle**, Co. Dublin. Tel: 01 904207.
**Clontarf**, Co. Dublin. Tel: 01 311305.
**County Louth**, Co. Louth. Tel: (041) 22327.
**Dublin and County**, Co. Dublin. Tel: 01 45217.
**Dundalk**, Co. Louth. Tel: (042) 32731.
**Four Lakes**, Co. Kildare. Tel: (045) 66003.
**Foxrock**, Co. Dublin. Tel: 01 893992.
**Greystones**, Co. Wicklow. Tel: 01 874614.
**Portmarnock**, Co. Dublin. Tel: 01 323082.
**Royal Dublin**, Bull Island, Co. Dublin. Tel: 01 337153.
**Royal Tara**, Co. Meath. Tel: (046) 25244.

**Skerries**, Co. Dublin. Tel: 01 491204.
**The Island**, Co. Dublin. Tel: 01 450595.

## The south-east
**Athlone**, Co. Westmeath. Tel: (0902) 2073.
**Carlow**, Co. Carlow. Tel: (0503) 31695.
**Clonmel**, Co. Tipperary. Tel: (052) 21183.
**Kilkenny**, Co. Kilkenny. Tel: (056) 22125.
**Mullingar**, Co. Westmeath. Tel: (044) 48366.
**Rosslare**, Co. Wexford. Tel: (053) 32113.
**Thurles**, Co. Tipperary. Tel: (0504) 21983.
**Tullamore**, Co. Offaly. Tel: (0506) 21439.
**Waterford**, Newrath, Waterford. Tel: (051) 76748.
**Wexford**, Mulgannon, Wexford. Tel: (053) 42238.

## The south-west
**Bandon**, Co. Cork. Tel: (023) 41111.
**Douglas**, Co. Cork. Tel: (021) 295297.
**Ennis**, Co. Clare. Tel: (065) 24074.
**Fermoy**, Co. Cork. Tel: (025) 31642.
**Monkstown**, Co. Cork. Tel: (021) 841376.

## The north-west
**Ballinasloe**, Co. Galway. Tel: (0905) 42126.
**Ballybofey and Stranorlar**, Co. Donegal. Tel: (074) 31093.
**Ballyliffen**, Co. Donegal. Tel: Clonmany 19.
**Bundoran** ,Co. Donegal. Tel: (072) 41302.
**Castlebar**, Co. Mayo. Tel: (094) 21649.
**Connemara**, Co. Galway. Tel: (095) 21153.
**County Cavan**, Co. Cavan. Tel: (049) 31283.
**County Sligo**, Co. Sligo. Tel: (071) 77186.
**Donegal**, Co. Donegal. Tel: (073) 34054.
**Enniscrone,** Co. Sligo. Tel: (096) 36297.
**Galway**, Co. Calway. Tel: (091) 23038.
**Letterkenny**, Co. Donegal. Tel: (074) 21150.
**North-West**, Co. Donegal. Tel: (074) 61027.
**Portsalon**, Co. Donegal. Tel: Portsalon 11.
**Westport**, Co. Mayo. Tel: (098) 25113.

# Useful information

## Golf package tour companies

Atlantic Golf,
54a Richmond Road,
Twickenham,
Middlesex.
Tel: 01 891 6451.

South West Ireland Golf Ltd,
5 Day Place,
Tralee,
Co. Kerry.
Tel: (066) 25733.

Golfing Holidays Northern Ireland,
Belfast Car Ferries,
Donegal Quay,
Belfast.
Tel: (0232) 220364.

Northern Irish Tourist Board,
River House,
High Street,
Belfast, BT1 2DS.
Tel: (0232) 231221.

Golfing Holidays,
Irish Tourist Board,
150 New Bond Street,
London, W1Y OAQ.
Tel: 01 493 3201.

# SPAIN

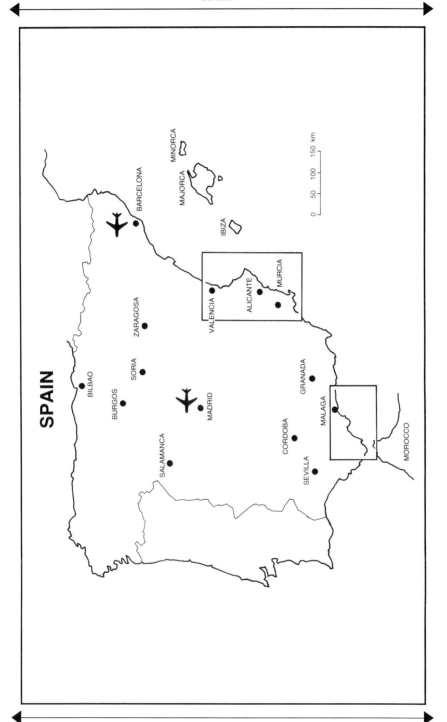

# THE COSTA DEL SOL

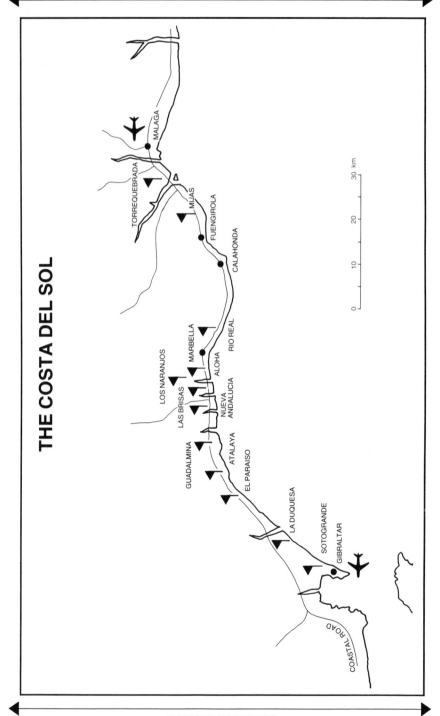

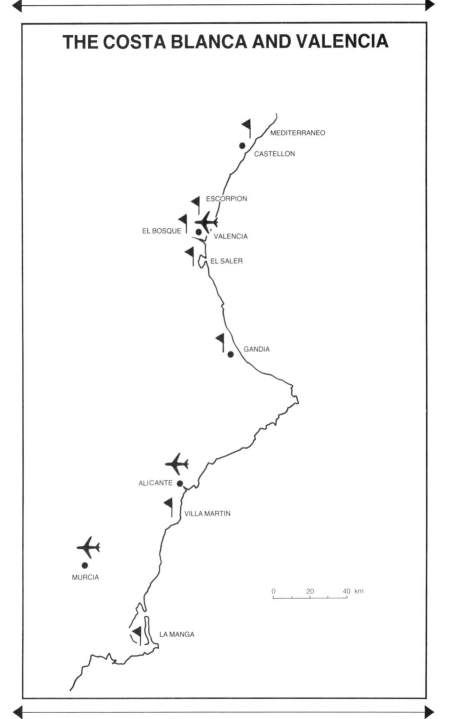

# THE COSTA BLANCA AND VALENCIA

MEDITERRANEO

CASTELLON

ESCORPION

EL BOSQUE

VALENCIA

EL SALER

GANDIA

ALICANTE

VILLA MARTIN

MURCIA

0    20    40  km

LA MANGA

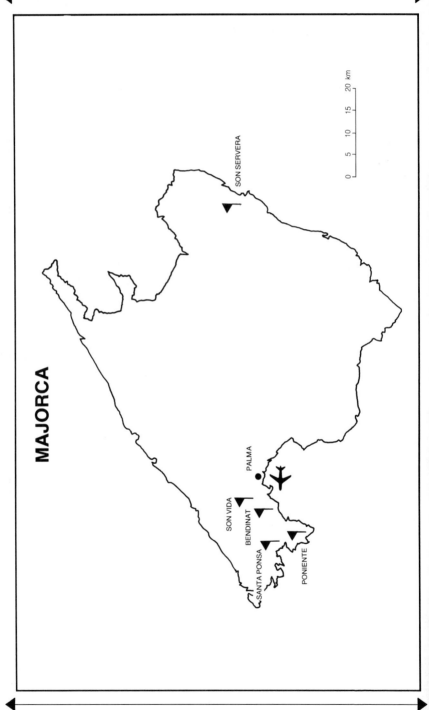

MAJORCA

SON SERVERA

PALMA

SON VIDA

BENDINAT

SANTA PONSA

PONIENTE

0   5   10   15   20 km

# Introduction

One of the first golf courses to be built in Spain was the Terramar Golf Club, some 40 kilometres from Barcelona and when it was opened in 1922 it hardly received a second glance from the locals. Malaga was the first club on the Costa Del Sol and was opened in 1925, while Pedrena, in the north of the country, about 24 kilometres from Santander, was opened in 1928. None of these caused so much as a raised eyebrow and they did little for the economy of a country that had other, more pressing problems to contend with. If crazy foreigners wished to spend money on barren land and spend good siesta time belting a small white ball all over the landscape it was their business and the locals got on with their own pursuits.

There were some people who discovered that these golfers were prepared to pay a few pesetas for anyone who would care to carry their golf clubs around 18 holes but even though the rewards of caddying were more than the average labourer earned for a week's work in the field there were still few takers. Spanish professionals came from the ranks of those caddies who persisted, but basically, golf was not recognised as a pastime by most Spaniards. It is well known elsewhere that the Pedrena course at Santander saw the emergence of Severiano Ballesteros as one of the greats in golf and that he was encouraged by relations who had already become professional golfers, but as far as the average Spaniard was concerned, no Sportsman who didn't play for either Real Madrid or Barcelona could be a national hero.

It was not until the 1960s and early 1970s that property developers saw what was to become a golfing revolution. Not that they had any altruistic thoughts about the furtherance of golf but what they did see was the undeniable attraction of a golf course as the centrepiece of their developments. The one priceless commodity was sunshine, and Spain had plenty to spare.

# The Costa del Sol

## Selected Courses

### Nueva Andalucia

With the boom in tourism during the 1960s and 1970s, the building of golf courses of a calibre high enough to attract major championships started and one of the first of these was Nueva Andalucia. Designed by Robert Trent Jones and opened in 1968 it was part of a 2500-acre holiday and residential complex that has since been used for a number of major competitions including the World Cup in 1973, which attracted golfers like Jack Nicklaus and Johnny Miller who were the winners on that occasion.

Nueva Andalucia, with large bunkers and numerous water hazards and typical Trent Jones undulating greens is a tough test for the scratch golfer but with forward tees and differing pin positions it also provides enjoyable golf for the long handicap holiday golfer. The golf course is built in a valley which opens out towards the sea from the Sierra Blanca mountains and the clubhouse is sited on high ground which overlooks the entire course. There is virtually no rough to speak of but plenty of sand and water to trap the unwary. There is a liberal sprinkling of pine trees, eucalyptus, palm, almond, fig and orange trees and in the middle distance, acre upon acre of sugar cane.

One of the more pleasing sights to me on the approach to the area from the direction of Marbella is the early morning clouds which hang around the top of the mountains like an ermine wrap around the throat of a beautiful woman. There are so many good holes that it would be presumptuous of me to choose what I consider are the outstanding ones. The general consensus of opinion is that the 2nd and the 12th are the best on the layout but golfing holes, like beauty itself, lie in the eye of the beholder.

**Location:** Eight kilometres from Marbella.
**Telephone:** (952) 812840.
**Length:** 6815 yards.
**Par:** 72.
**Accommodation:** The Costa Del Sol abounds with hotel accommodation, as well as villas and apartments.

# Sotogrande

Sotogrande, was Trent Jones's first venture in Europe. It is twenty-three miles from Gibraltar and the Old Course was opened in 1965.

The greens are large and the tees are very long, some think excessively so, but they do allow for variations in pin placement and in the length of the holes. The contours of the greens are typical Trent Jones and the brilliant white crushed marble in the bunkers adds a suitable frame to the picture. Yet another 'first' at Sotogrande was the use of Bermuda grass on the fairways and it was also sown on some greens but was soon replaced there with a variety of bent grass.

The sea plays no part in the playing of Sotogrande but merely acts as an attractive backcloth to the course. The fertile valley of the Guadiaro River, the dark green of the trees and the outline of the sierras adds to the intrinsic beauty, and the lasting impression that I got on my first visit was how similar it was to some of the British courses.

The architect once described a golf course as a battleground. 'The players attack the course,' he said, 'and it is the architect's job to defend it.' Robert Trent Jones certainly does that.

Sotogrande New Course was opened in 1975 and there have been many discussions as to whether it matches the subtle qualities of the Old Course. It is of similar length and shares the same rolling landscape. To me there is greater premium placed on the drive and the greens seem less of a problem than on the Old but perhaps I had one of those days that all golfers have from time to time.

Sotogrande may be the golfing pearl of Spain, but it required a long journey from Malaga Airport along a coast road that was described as 'the most dangerous road in Europe'. Now, however, it can be reached from Gibraltar with scheduled flights from London and Manchester and excellent package golfing holidays through Sovereign Golf – a subsidiary of British Airways – who also cater for most, if not all, of the golf courses in Spain.

**Location:** Thirty-seven kilometres from Gibraltar.
**Telephone:** (956) 792029.
**Length:** Old Course: 5885 metres. New Course: 6263 metres.
**SSS:** Old Course: 72. New Course: 72.
**Accommodation:** See Nueva Andalucia, p. 56.

## Torrequebrada

For my holiday golf, despite the obvious attractions of Sotogrande, I turn from Malaga Airport towards Torremolinos on the coast road which is clearly signposted from the airport and then on towards Fuengirola. Near Torremolinos is Torrequebrada, a course for those of you who are looking for a really tough start to your golfing holiday.

This is, in my opinion, one of the most demanding courses on the Costa del Sol and is not helpful for the long handicap golfer who is looking for a nice relaxing round. A very good golf course laid out on hilly terrain, it does nothing for weak legs and a suspect golf swing!

**Location:** Near Torremolinos.
**Telephone:** 442742.
**Length:** 6385 yards.
**Par:** 72.
**Accommodation:** See Nueva Andalucia, p. 56.

## Mijas

For holiday golf at its most relaxing take a short trip from Fuengirola to this 36-hole complex. There you will find Los Olivos –

Playing Los Olivos course at Mijas the easy way

The Olives – and Los Lagos – The Lakes – both of which I found to be most enjoyable and certainly among the cheapest in this neck of the Costa del Sol.

There are some very good holes on both of these courses and due allowance is made for the holiday golfer from the forward tees. The Olives was opened in 1976 and The Lakes some ten years later. One or two of the holes on the back nine on The Lakes are quite hilly and scenically, without peer with small greens and well placed bunkers.

**Location:** Four kilometres from Fuengirola.
**Telephone:** 476843.
**Length:** Los Olivos: 5896 metres. Los Lagos: 6348 metres.
**SSS:** Los Olivos: 71. Los Lagos: 73.
**Accommodation:** See Nueva Andalucia, p. 56.

# Rio Real

Rio Real is a most attractive golf course that was opened in 1965. Now fully matured and well used by holiday golfers it is more expensive than Mijas and is one of the few courses in this area that so far does not have golf carts for hire. And although there are some

The mature and attractive Rio Real course

who will say that golf was meant to be played on foot the additional fee for the hire of a cart is well worth the money and does save weary limbs in extremes of heat.

The Rio Real River features in many of the holes and there are one or two steep climbs from one green to the next tee. This may be why they do not have carts as yet.

**Location:** Between Fuengirola and Marbella, just beyond Calahonda.
**Telephone:** 771700.
**Length:** 6130 metres.
**SSS:** 72.
**Accommodation:** The Los Monteros Hotel is opposite the entrance, and there are any number of villas and apartments.

## Aloha

On the other side of Marbella is the first of another group of courses. Aloha, an 18-hole layout was opened in 1975 and like all of the golf courses in this area is always in first class condition. It is a difficult driving course with sloping fairways and a number of dog-leg holes to boot.

The Aloha course has many attractive features and is always in first-class condition

**Location:** Eight kilometres from Marbella.
**Telephone:** 813750.
**Length:** 6887 yards.
**SSS:** 72.
**Accommodation:** See Nueva Andalucia, p. 56.

## Los Naranjos

Close to Aloha, this is one of the longer courses in this area, with plenty of variety. Laid out between orange groves and stands of tall eucalyptus trees, it often plays longer than its par 72 suggests.

**Location:** Eight kilometres from Marbella.
**Telephone:** 815206.
**Length:** 7073 yards.
**Par:** 72.
**Accommodation:** See Nueva Andalucia, p. 56.

## Las Brisas

Leave both the Aloha and Los Naranjos courses, turn right, and quite soon you will see the entrance to this course. Las Brisas is considered by many to be the finest golf course in Spain and whilst I do not agree entirely, it is a very good course from the front and from the back tees and can be enjoyed by the long, medium and short handicap golfer. The greens can be extremely tricky when the groundstaff set the mower blades on the mean side and even when they do not, there are many subtle borrows that will tax the patience of all but the good putters. The water hazards are well placed and correct club selection is of the utmost importance.

**Location:** Eight kilometres from Marbella.
**Telephone:** 810875.
**Length:** 6198 metres.
**SSS:** 73.
**Accommodation:** See Nueva Andalucia, p. 56.

## Guadalmina

This course is just a little further on from Las Brisas on the road to Gibraltar and has two 18-hole courses. It was one of the earlier complexes to open in Spain and is a most pleasant spot to play. When I was last there a number of the holes were getting a

Recently rejuvenated, the Guadalmina course offers the welcome facility of an extra clubhouse at the 9th

welcome face-lift. Greens and tees were being relaid and the fairways were being rejuvenated. Both golf courses provide enjoyable holiday golf and the holes that border on the sea with the 'extra' clubhouse at the 9th, which has excellent food and service, are as pleasing as any that I have played. There is nothing more pleasant, to my way of thinking, than to play the first nine holes before the weather becomes too hot and then to stop for a leisurely lunch – the local fish is first rate – before tackling the back nine holes in the relative cool of the late afternoon in true holiday style. In fact, if you take your holiday between the middle of May and the end of September it is always advisable – and certainly more enjoyable – to avoid the extreme heat of the noonday sun by taking a long and leisurely lunch after the first nine holes.

**Location:** Sixty-eight kilometres from Marbella Airport.
**Telephone:** 781317.
**Length:** First course: 6060 metres. Second course: 6200 metres.
**SSS:** First course: 72. Second course: 72.
**Accommodation:** The Golf Hotel is a pleasant place to stay, and there are villas and apartments.

# Atalaya Park

Atalaya Park Golf Course was opened in 1967. Its 18-hole layout suffered, in its early stages, from too much golf and in my opinion, lack of good green-keeping but this situation has since been rectified and it has recently had a complete and vigorous face-lift. It is a most enjoyable parkland-type layout and an ideal venue for the casual, holiday golfer.

**Location:** About ten kilometres west of Marbella.
**Telephone:** 781894.
**Length:** 6272 metres.
**SSS:** 73.
**Accommodation:** See Nueva Andalucia, p. 56.

# El Paraiso

This course was opened for play in 1974. The 18-hole course has superb greens with generous rolling fairways and has a beautiful setting which is complemented by a proliferation of trees and shrubs.

The elegant 18-hole course at El Paraiso

**Location:** About fourteen kilometres west of Marbella.
**Telephone:** 784716.
**Length:** 5690 metres.
**Par:** 72.
**Accommodation:** See Nueva Andalucia, p. 56.

## La Duquesa

The most recent addition to the Costa del Sol courses is laid out on undulating ground with some lovely views of the sea and presents the latest exciting golfing challenge to the holiday golfer.

**Location:** Halfway between Estepona and Sotogrande.
**Telephone:** 890425/6.
**Length:** 6756 yards.
**Par:** 72.
**Accommodation:** See Nueva Andalucia, p. 56.

# The Costa Blanca

## Introduction

When I first visited the eastern side of the Iberian Peninsula there were no golf courses and there may well be some who suggest that it was all the better for that oversight!

It was also known as the Costa Blanca – the White Coast – but from recent brochures that fall on my desk I see that the area concerned is now sometimes called the Costa Calida. The main airport which serves this part of Spain is Alicante.

## Selected Courses

### La Manga

La Manga Campo de Golf as it was then known was the brainchild of one Gregory Peters, an expatriate American who had made a personal fortune from his furniture and leather factories elsewhere in Spain. Based in Madrid, Peters was looking for a small piece of land on which to build a modest, 9-hole golf course for his golfing

La Manga 36-hole complex, which contains all necessary ingredients for a successful sporting holiday

friends and some seven years after he commenced his search he was told of La Manga. At that time in the late 1960s this area was not known to holidaymakers.

When La Manga was opened in 1972 it was the first 36-hole complex in Spain and was written of as the most luxurious development in Europe. In addition to the 36-hole complex there were some 1100 acres of estate which were bordered on three sides by the mountains with views on the open side across the distant Mar Menor (an inland lake some fifteen miles long) and the Mediterranean. The inaugural Pro/Am in 1972 was a glittering occasion and the prize money on offer to the professionals was, at £25,000, the richest in Europe. Heads of state mingled and played golf with crown princes and film stars whilst professionals like Arnold Palmer, Gary Player and Billy Casper trod the fairways of the North and South Courses.

The club was host to the Spanish Open for five years and the tennis complex was under the guidance of Manuel Santana. The development went through a series of financial hiccups and was later purchased by its present owners, European Car Ferries, and is now rapidly fulfilling its initial potential as a sporting complex.

There are direct flights from Gatwick during the season to Murcia Airport, which is a Spanish Air Force base, and Murcia can

Gary Player at La Manga

also be reached by air during the high season direct from Madrid. The main international airport, however, is Alicante. From Murcia it is but a twenty-minute drive to La Manga Club but from Alicante it is a good hour and a half.

In addition to the golf, there is a David Lloyd Racquet Club, an equestrian centre and a cricket pitch. The temperatures all year round are ideal for golf and visitors will find all the facilities they require in the tasteful Spanish style, self-contained villages which include supermarkets, hairdressers, restaurants and a medical centre. If you require an alternative to golf, the nearby Mar Menor is ideal for sailing, water skiing and other water sports and there is a casino on the La Manga strip.

Of the two golf courses the most demanding of the two is the South Course. This is a championship layout and many of the holes feature a barranca which snakes through both courses. Huge greens are complemented by very long tees and one needs a handicap of 21 or less for men and 27 or less for ladies in order to play this course. The PGA European Tour School holds its qualifying session on both North and South Courses during late November and early December and both courses are closed on these days until 3.00 PM, so it is advisable to check with your travel agent or the Club before you book.

The recurring problem on the South Course, even for short handicap golfers, is underclubbing on shots to the greens. A pin position to the back of some of these enormous greens can make a difference of two and sometimes three clubs, so be warned!

The North Course is the shorter of the two but to my mind, not only is it the more picturesque but it is also a better test of golf even from the forward tees and in consequence, the more enjoyable for holiday golf. The fairways are lined with palm trees – as are those of the South Course – and there is little or no rough to speak of so searching for lost balls, except in some of the barrancas, is not a problem. There are also a number of lakes which come into play, both off the tee and for second and sometimes approach shots to the green, so if your ball lands in one of these you can put it down to experience!

**Location:** Los Bellones, Cartagena, Murcia.
**Telephone:** (968) 563 3500.
**Length:** South Course: 6855 yards. North Course: 6445 yards.
**SSS:** South Course: 72. North Course: 70.
**Accommodation:** There is a hotel adjoining the clubhouse and numerous first-class villas and apartments. Another hotel is under construction.

## Villa Martin

Villa Martin was opened in 1972. It is about a twenty-minute drive from La Manga Club and is a typical holiday, play-for-fun course with 18 holes of pleasant golf with a number of 'blind' tee shots that require accuracy and length. A small and friendly clubhouse provides good food and excellent service.

**Location:** Just off the main Alicante–La Manga road.
**Telephone:** 320384.
**Information for Visitors:** It is advisable to book by telephone before travelling to the course.
**Length:** 5899 metres.
**SSS:** 72.

# Valencia

## Selected Courses

### Mediterraneo

This is an 18-hole course which is set in a valley and surrounded by mountains. It was opened in 1978 and is now a well matured test of golf. The fairways are lined by olive trees and flowering shrubs and the water hazards add to the beauty of what has been described as a 'little golfing gem'. The modern clubhouse provides excellent food and first class service and facilities.

**Location:** La Coma Borriol, Castellon.
**Telephone:** (964) 321227.
**Length:** 6038 metres.
**Par:** 71.

### El Saler

El Saler was rated in a recent survey as one of the top thirty golf courses in the world. It is certainly a true test of the best of golfers and has a pleasing mixture of holes, some tree-lined and others links-style. The course is always in excellent condition and the attendant facilities are good.

**Location:** Eighteen kilometres from Valencia.
**Telephone:** 3236850.
**Length:** 7133 yards.
**Par:** 72.
**Accommodation:** The Parador Luis Vives is situated on the course.

### Escorpion

This is another lovely 18-hole course, with an abundance of orange and olive groves that blend pleasingly with a beautifully modernised Spanish farmhouse.

**Location:** Betera, twenty kilometres from Valencia.
**Telephone:** 1601211.

**Length:** 6980 yards.
**Par:** 72.

## El Bosque

This is the most recent and exciting addition to the Valencia golf scene and was originally designed by Robert Trent Jones. It is back in the mountains and within easy reach of Valencia. The new owners have carried out extensive work on the course which will be a worthy addition to golf in this region.

**Location:** En Chiva, Valencia.
**Telephone:** 3263800.
**Length:** 6040 metres.
**SSS:** 72.

# Other Regions

## Around Barcelona

### El Prat

One of the better known courses in this area, El Prat was opened in 1954. It has been used for many professional events and although on the short side, it is a good test of golf.

**Location:** Three kilometres from Barcelona Airport.
**Telephone:** (93) 3790278.
**Information for Visitors:** El Prat has a large private membership, and a telephone call is advisable before visiting the club.
**Length:** 5800 metres.
**SSS:** 72.

### San Cugat

**Location:** Fifteen kilometres from Barcelona.
**Telephone:** (93) 674390858.
**Information for Visitors:** This course is well used by locals, and a telephone call is advisable.
**Length:** 5085 metres.
**Par:** 70.

# On Majorca

## Santa Ponsa

Whilst the island of Majorca has been a firm favourite with holiday-makers who wanted a quiet place to bask in the sun, it is not generally associated with golf as is the Costa del Sol but, for all that, the island does have five golf courses, the best of which is probably Santa Ponsa. It has well-matured fairways and greens and provides an excellent test of golf.

**Location:** On the western side of the island, eighteen kilometres from Palma.
**Telephone:** (971) 690211/690800.
**Length:** 7093 yards.
**Par:** 72.
**Accommodation:** The Santa Ponsa Golf Hotel is close to the first tee, and the Hotel Club Galatzo is also close by. The Galatzo also offers five outdoor tennis courts, two indoor courts, one indoor and two outdoor pools, horse riding and saunas.

## Poniente

Slightly shorter than Santa Ponsa this is a course of great contrast. Many of the holes are played through tall pine trees and on plateau type fairways whilst other holes have much more open layouts with water hazards as well.

**Location:** Sixteen kilometres from Palma.
**Telephone:** (971) 223615.
**Length:** 6247 yards.
**SSS:** 72.

## Son Vida

This is the oldest course on the island and although it is considered short by modern standards, you will need to club each shot with great care.

**Location:** Five kilometres from Palma.
**Telephone:** (971) 237620.
**Length:** 6247 yards.
**Par:** 71.

## Son Servera

Situated in the north-east corner of Majorca, a 1¾ hour drive from Palma, this is a small 9-hole course of modest length. It provides an interesting and varied game of golf for the more leisurely golfer and if it is peace you require, then this is the spot.

**Location:** Seventy kilometres from Palma.
**Telephone:** (971) 567802.
**Length:** 5840 metres.
**SSS:** 72.

## Bendinat

The newest course on this most pleasant island is this 9-hole course, with an excellent clubhouse and a golf course for the true holiday golfer.

**Location:** Near the resort of Cala Mayor.
**Length:** 3230 yards.
**Par:** 34.

# On Gran Canaria

## Club de Golf de Las Palmas–Bandama

Gran Canaria is one of the seven canary islands which lie close to the west coast of Africa and the Club de Golf de Las Palmas is Spain's oldest golf club. The championship course is on the peak of a volcanic crater and has narrow, tree-lined fairways, fast greens and beautiful scenery. The weather is always superb and there are vivid contrasts in scenery from verdant green forests, barren expanses of desert, long golden beaches to spectacular volcanic peaks.

**Location:** Bandama, fourteen kilometres from Las Palmas.
**Telephone:** 351050/350104.
**Length:** 6259 yards.
**Par:** 71.

**Accommodation:** The Hotel Golf Bandama is a small hotel with first-class personal service and good facilities. Hotel guests are given temporary membership of the golf course and can participate in most of the competitions.

# Useful Information

## Spanish Golf Association

Federacion Espanola de Golf,
9-3 Dacha,
Madrid 20,
Spain.

## Golf package tour companies

Longshot Golf Holidays by Meon,
Meon House,
College St.,
Petersfield,
Hants, GU32 3JN.
Tel: (0730) 66561.

Sovereign Golf (British Airways),
P.O. Box 100,
Hodford House,
17-27 High St,
Hounslow,
Middx, TW3 1TB.
Tel: 01 748 7559
(Manchester) (061) 927 7090
(Glasgow) (041) 248 3191.

Sky Golf Holidays,
327 Lincoln Rd,
Peterborough, PE1 2PF.
Tel: (0733) 67434.

Atalya Aparta Golf (Apartments),
11 Longfield,
Little Kingshill, Great Missenden,
Bucks.
Tel: (02 406) 4856.

Reduced green fees are available with package tour bookings. As an individual visitor you will find that the green fees are much higher than those on offer from the tour operators in their package deals.

# PORTUGAL

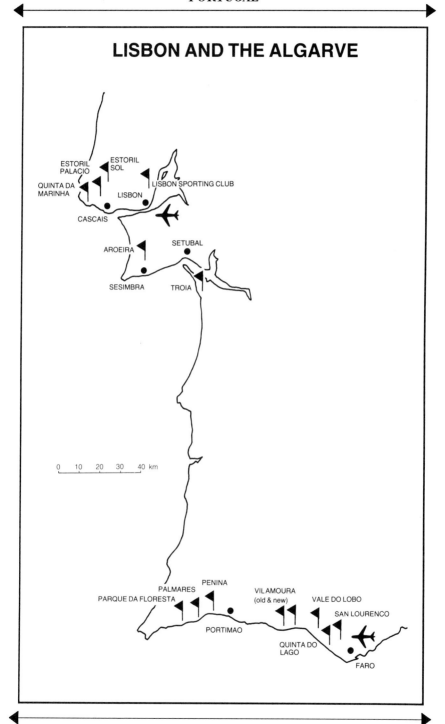

# LISBON AND THE ALGARVE

ESTORIL
PALACIO
ESTORIL
SOL
QUINTA DA
MARINHA
LISBON SPORTING CLUB
LISBON
CASCAIS
AROEIRA
SETUBAL
SESIMBRA
TROIA

0   10   20   30   40 km

PALMARES
PENINA
VILAMOURA
(old & new)
VALE DO LOBO
PARQUE DA FLORESTA
SAN LOURENCO
PORTIMAO
QUINTA DO
LAGO
FARO

# The Algarve

## Introduction

There are many beautiful parts of the world that are eventually ruined by people whilst a few still retain the character of centuries past. The lovely Algarve coast was known to only a few selective travellers who returned each year to delight in the long stretches of pristine white beaches, red cliffs and orange, fig and olive trees. Hot sun and cooling Atlantic breezes with low humidity made the Algarve an idyllic holiday venue, and it soon became popular, while still retaining its charm.

It is surprising therefore that the first golf course on this gorgeous stretch was not constructed until the 1960s. Now it offers some outstanding golf.

## Selected Courses

### Vilamoura

One of the earliest courses in this area, Vilamoura was part of a 4000-acre development plan and the golf course which was designed by Frank Pennink was opened for play in 1969. In many respects, even off the forward tees, it was a tough challenge that was not always appreciated by the average holiday golfer.

Vilamoura now has two good 18-hole courses, Vilamoura 1 and Vilamoura 2. Vilamoura 1, the first Pennink creation, is always in first-class condition. The steeply sloping land is covered with umbrella pine trees that are suitably placed to add to the attraction – and difficulty – of the holes and, as many a golfer has found to his cost, these trees seem to gobble up stray golf balls like a venus fly trap! It has a well appointed clubhouse with an English professional and English-speaking staff in most areas.

The 18 holes are quite separate with undulating fairways and little or no rough to speak of especially underneath the umbrella pines. Despite its close proximity to Faro Airport there is always a feeling of secluded isolation and it is an ideal golfing holiday venue. My old friend Bernard Hunt once described Vilamoura as 'the hardest golf course in Portugal' and as he won the Algarve Open there, few who have played the course will disagree.

Challenging golf in attractive surroundings is the appeal of both courses at Vilamoura

Vilamoura 2 was recently redesigned to the specifications of Robert Trent Jones and is a most enjoyable test of golf.

**Location:** Twenty-five kilometres west of Faro Airport.
**Telephone:** 65275/7.
**Length:** Vilamoura 1: 6700 yards. Vilamoura 2: 6294 yards.
**Par:** Vilamoura 1: 72. Vilamoura 2: 73.
**Accommodation:** There are numerous first-class hotels in the vicinity, with many villas and apartments to rent. The Hotel Dona Filipa is possibly my favourite, but the Dom Pedro is equally acceptable.

## Quinta do Lago

A more recent addition in these parts, this is now considered by many to be one of the finest championship courses in Europe and has hosted the Portuguese Open on a number of occasions. It has a 9 and an 18-hole layout. Both courses are always in immaculate condition and it is a most enjoyable spot to play and relax.
**Location:** Twenty kilometres from Faro.
**Telephone:** 93459.
**Length:** 18-hole course: 6941 yards. 9-hole course: 3140 yards.
**Par:** 18-hole course: 72. 9-hole course: 35.

Quinta do Lago – a fine championship course and frequent host to the Portuguese Open

# Vale do Lobo

This course also has an 18 and a 9-hole layout, and was originally designed by Henry Cotton. There have been a number of alterations over the past years which have only added to the golfer's pleasure and the 7th hole, with the Atlantic on the golfer's left and a green situated on the other side of the cliff-edge, like the 9th at Turnberry, Scotland, is possibly one of the most photographed holes in golf.

Were I to be hypercritical I would say that there are too many villas in close proximity to some of the holes but this may only be because on one occasion, after the mildest of off-line shots, I was forced to retrieve my golf ball from a swimming pool alongside one of the villas!

**Location:** Nineteen kilometres from Faro.
**Telephone:** Almancil 94137.
**Length:** 18-hole course: 6808 yards. 9-hole course: 3027 yards.
**Par:** 18-hole course: 72. 9-hole course: 35.

# Penina

This is yet another of the Henry Cotton-designed challenges, with a championship course and a 9-hole course. This was home to Henry

The Penina Hotel

Cotton and his late wife, Toots, and the new owners, Trusthouse Forte have given the championship course a welcome face-lift.

**Location:** About five kilometres from Portimao and about an hour's drive from Faro Airport.
**Telephone:** 22051/9.
**Length:** Championship course: 6889 yards. 9-hole course: 3251 yards.
**Par:** Championship course: 73. 9-hole course: 36.
**Accommodation:** The hotel overlooking the course boasts an international cuisine, first class service and excellent facilities, including sauna, olympic pool, snooker, bowls, tennis and aquatic sports.

## Palmares

Situated towards the far end of the Algarve coastline this course offers a combination of links and parkland golf.
**Location:** Five kilometres from Lagos.
**Telephone:** 62961.
**Length:** 6615 yards.
**Par:** 71.

## Parque da Floresta

Another new course opened for play in 1987, Parque da Floresta is situated to the west of Palmares and also overlooks the sea.
**Location:** About 24 kilometres west of Lagos.
**Telephone:** (0826) 5407.
**Length:** 6360 yards.
**Par:** 72.

## San Lourenco

This is the most recent addition to golf in this part of Portugal and is quite close to Quinta Do Lago. The designers have made good use of the natural lakes on this superb layout and it is due to be opened for play in late 1988. However, at the time of writing it is only open to guests of the Dona Filipa and Penina Hotels.

**Location:** On the Quinta do Lago estate.
**Telephone:** not yet available.
**Length:** 6600 yards.
**Par:** 72.

**Accommodation:** There will be 96 apartments which overlook the golf course and they should be opened at the same time as the golf course.

# Lisbon

# Introduction

Lisbon, in the north of Portugal, has long been a popular venue for golfers from Britain and the six excellent courses are divided into two golfing centres, Estoril and the Costa Azul. The two centres are but an hour's journey by road apart and the first-class coastal roads provide some spectacular views of the ocean and a trip over the impressive suspension bridge.

A special 'Lisbon Golf Pack' is offered by Sovereign Golf which entitles the holder to play golf at both centres with special green fee arrangements. The city of Lisbon has some excellent restaurants and with its uncrowded golf courses is an ideal venue for both summer and winter golf.

# Selected Courses

## Lisbon Sporting Club

This is one of the oldest courses in Portugal and was opened in 1922. It is situated in a forestry reserve and although there are only 14 holes the last 4 are replayed to complete the 18. It is a very pleasant golf course set in beautiful surroundings and you will need to polish up your driving to card a good score.

**Location:** Twenty kilometres east of Lisbon.
**Telephone:** Belas 960077.
**Length:** 5800 yards.
**Par:** 69.

## Quinta da Marinha

Where would golf be without the stamp of Robert Trent Jones? This layout of the world famous architect is the latest addition to golf in the Lisbon area and with its dramatic design and panoramic views is a first-class and enjoyable test of golf.

**Location:** Thirty-two kilometres east of Lisbon.
**Telephone:** 289008/289388.
**Length:** 6600 yards.
**Par:** 71.

## Troia

The venue for the Portuguese Open in 1982, this 18-hole course with its tight fairways and small greens proved to be a worthy challenge to the professional golfers and from the forward tees, if slightly less severe, presents an equally rewarding challenge to the handicap golfer.

**Location:** Forty-eight kilometres from Lisbon.
**Telephone:** 44151/44236.
**Length:** 6627 yards.
**Par:** 72.

## Aroeira

This 18-hole course was designed by Frank Pennink. Each hole is cut through a dense forest and lined with huge fir trees. For a championship course of this calibre it is not crowded and there is a an American flavour about the large greens and bunkers. There are several water holes and although the rolling fairways are tree-lined one never has the feeling of being hemmed in.

**Location:** 18 miles south of Lisbon.
**Telephone:** not available.
**Length:** 6890 yards.
**Par:** 69.

# Estoril Palacio

There is an 18-hole, and a 9-hole course, both of which provide excellent holiday golf. There is a premium on accuracy rather than length and the course hosted the 1987 Portuguese Open.
**Location:** Two kilometres from Estoril.
**Telephone:** 2680176.
**Length:** 18-hole course: 5926 yards. 9-hole course: 2621 yards.
**Par:** 18-hole course: 69. 9-hole course: 32.

# Estoril Sol

This pleasant 9-hole course is played from 18 separate tees and will

The Estoril Palacio courses offer a demanding test of golfing accuracy

test the skills of most handicap golfers. Being shorter, it will leave the golfer feeling less tired than other venues and the premium is on subtlety rather than strength.

**Location:** Seven kilometres north of Estoril.
**Telephone:** 9232461.
**Length:** 4426 yards.
**Par:** 66.

# Useful Information

## Golf package tour companies

Longshot Golf Holidays (see SPAIN, p. 72)
Sky Golf Holidays (see SPAIN, p. 72)
Sovereign Golf (see SPAIN, p. 72)

Green fees are increased yearly and for the individual golfer can be quite high.
Green fees at a greatly reduced rate and guaranteed starting times are available through the golfing tour operators.

# MOROCCO

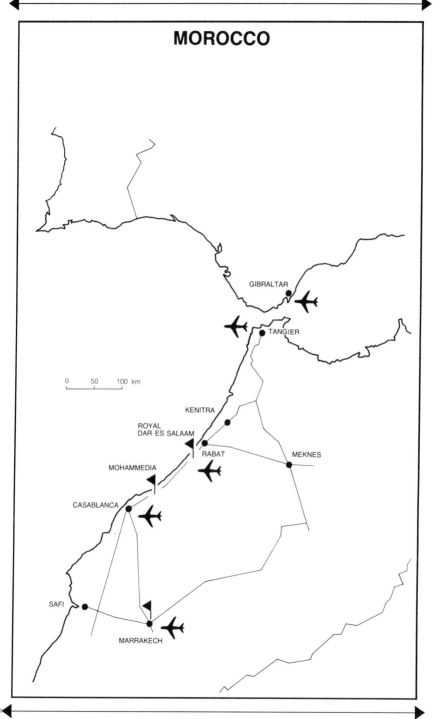

# MOROCCO

GIBRALTAR

TANGIER

0  50  100 km

KENITRA

ROYAL
DAR ES SALAAM

RABAT

MEKNES

MOHAMMEDIA

CASABLANCA

SAFI

MARRAKECH

# Introduction

My first glimpse of Morocco was from the front seat of a cinema. As far as I was concerned then, it was a land of swaying palm trees, snorting camels, yashmaks, a casbah, Bing Crosby, Bob Hope and Dorothy Lamour. The Morocco of today bears little resemblance to the pictures that were conjured up by the movie-makers in those far-off days but it is certainly a land of great contrast, and the winter temperatures make it an ideal spot for golf.

Viewed from the window of an aeroplane on the flight to Casablanca airport there are acres of neat, green squares that give some indication of the local agriculture. On the ground a different scenario unfolds. There are areas that are as clean and as modern as one would wish to find and, in direct contrast, roadside camps that house scrawny camels, miserable-looking livestock and people that appear to exist on nothing.

My driver on one visit was a burnous-clad, bearded version of Nigel Mansell, who drove with all the skill and panache of a demented flea. He had the reactions of some of the tree-climbing goats that we saw en route to our hotel and none of their dexterity. On

Marrakech golf course – well designed but not maintained to the highest standard

the road to the capital city of Rabat our car was waved off the road by a couple of gun-toting traffic cops who were escorting a convoy of large, black Mercedes that contained a number of Russian diplomats. Our driver explained that in a situation such as this it was better to keep well out of the way as the police gentlemen operated on a short fuse! And although this was not part of an inclusive tourist package it gave some indication of the muted respect in which the common man held the upholders of law and order in Morocco!

There are a number of golf courses in Morocco. An 18-hole layout on the outskirts of Marrakech still bore the signs of a skilled designer when I was there, although it lacked rudimentary maintenance – water and fertilizer – and the majority of its fairways were covered in weeds of all shapes and sizes. The greens were not a great deal better and similar inspections of courses in Casablanca and Tangier made me wonder if Humphrey Bogart was thinking of golf when he uttered those immortal lines, 'Play it again, Sam.'

# Selected Courses

## Royal Dar Es Salaam

This is a golfing complex fit for a king – King Hassan II of Morocco, one of the most enthusiastic of golfing royals. Robert Trent Jones was commissioned to lay out his gem of a course which wends its picturesque way through a large cork forest.

The Red Course was completed in 1971 and is a long course by anyone's standards. It includes huge tees, undulating greens and beautifully sculpted bunkers together with water hazards and cunningly sloped fairways.

It has always been my opinion that Robert Trent Jones did not like golfers and the sloping greens, which, unless hit in the perfect spot throw the ball into a waiting bunker, are typical of his designs. If some of the water hazards do not actually encroach on the target area they are so placed as to intrude in the golfer's sight-line when he is contemplating the next shot.

There is just as much potential as actual danger on a Trent Jones golf course and many of his more subtle ploys are in evidence here. The mere sight of water seems to make the average golfer tighten his grip, to raise the blood pressure and make the normal act of breathing a major problem. A slow, elegant swing gets

The 9th hole of the Red Course at the Royal Dar es Salaam golf course – a problematic par 3

quicker and shorter and the simple mechanics of returning the club-head to the ball becomes a physical and mental challenge.

Such a hole is the par 3, 199-yard 9th on the Red Course. It is also one of the most picturesque holes to be found anywhere in the world. The tee is on the bank of a large lake and the green, a small island dot in the middle of this expanse of water looks much farther and most golfers, seeing this hole for the first time, will refer to their scorecard again to check the distance. It has been suggested that it was measured by a drunken snake-charmer but whilst the holiday golfer will play a casual 6 or 7 iron to the heart of the green and stroll across two Chinese-style wooden bridges which connect the green with the mainland, the more serious player, playing from the back tee, will be reaching for a long iron and, when the wind is against him, possibly a driver. Unlike his less-gifted brother, he will not pause to admire the exotic wildfowl – flamingos, geese and all manner of ducks – but will consider the plight of a well-known tournament professional who was so obsessed with his idea of how the hole should be played that he hit six balls into the water and finished up with a 14 on his card.

I was told of another incident at this hole which involved a group of visiting Americans. They had all failed to negotiate the lake during their morning round and, after a liquid lunch, they returned to tackle the hole once more. Some 200 new balls later they returned to the clubhouse and had still not hit the green, which, as the assistant pro said to me, was good for his sale of golf balls but bad for their egos.

The condition of this jewel in the crown can only be described as superlative and it is little wonder when on considers that whilst the average golf course can cope quite well with about 12 ground staff this one keeps 500 men in menial employment. Each bunker has its own custodian who spends his day sitting in the shade of the cork trees, only appearing after the golfer has walked away, to restore his bunker to its former pristine glory.

Both the nearby Blue and Green Courses are kept in the same condition and remind me in parts of an amalgam of some of the holes at the Berkshire, Worplesdon and West Hill.

The long, low clubhouse is strikingly modern with floodlit fountains, sunken gardens that are a blaze of colour and a large bar with leather decor. The dining room has an international cuisine, first-class service, and a selection of cheeses the like of which I have never seen elsewhere. Suede-faced lockers in the changing rooms are complemented by individual bathrooms and attendants who would not be out of place on an up-market health farm. The tired golfer could be excused for spending as much time in here as out on the golf course!

**Location:** At Dar es Salaam, near Rabat.

**Information for Visitors:** Closed on Mondays. In addition, the Red Course is closed for a two-week period in November and again in March for major tournaments. It could also be closed for half a day or so from time to time when King Hassan arrives to play. The maximum handicap allowed for men on the Red Course is 18, and for ladies 24. On the Blue and Green Courses, the maximum handicaps allowed are 24 for men and 32 for ladies. Caddies are compulsory on the Red Course, but are very reasonable.

**Length:** Red Course: 7462 yards. Blue Course: 6450 yards, 18 holes. Green Course: 2266 yards, 9 holes.

**Par:** Red Course, 73; Blue Course, 72; Green Course, 32.

**Accommodation:** The nearest hotel to the Royal Dar es Salaam course is the Hyatt Regency (formerly a Hilton), a watering hole that includes a free shuttle bus to and from the golf course and to various locations in Rabat.

# Mohammedia

A pleasant, well-established 18-hole layout.

**Location:** Twenty-five kilometres from Casablanca.
**Information for Visitors:** Closed on Tuesdays. Caddies are compulsory, but very reasonable.
**Length:** 6634 yards.
**Par:** 72.
**Accommodation:** The Miramar Hotel is a two-minute drive away, and offers free golf to residents.

# Marrakech

Another pleasant spot to play a few leisurely holes but although the design of the course is excellent it is not maintained to the same high standards as some of the others.

**Accommodation:** The Mamounia Hotel is one of the best in Morocco and was a favourite haunt of Sir Winston Churchill and other distinguished travellers. It has recently undergone extensive refurbishment but still retains all of the traditional Moorish architectural features.

A favourite haunt of Winston Churchill, the Mamounia Hotel in Marrakech

# Useful Information

## Golf package tour companies

Excellent value for money golfing packages are offered by Longshot Golf Holidays (see SPAIN, p. 72).

# DENMARK

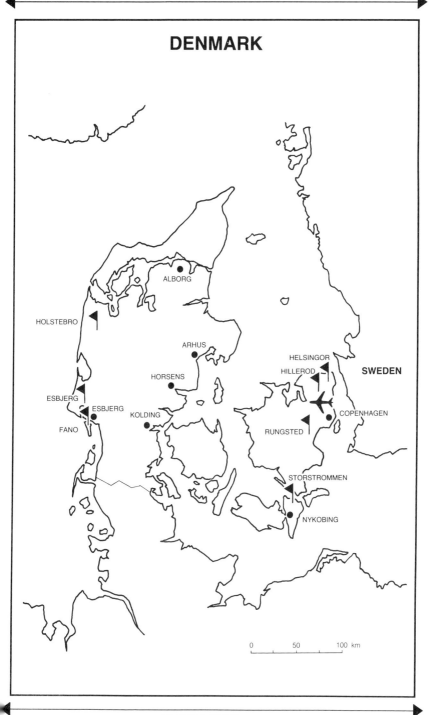

# DENMARK

ALBORG

HOLSTEBRO

ARHUS

HELSINGOR

HILLEROD

**SWEDEN**

HORSENS

ESBJERG

ESBJERG

KOLDING

COPENHAGEN

FANO

RUNGSTED

STORSTROMMEN

NYKOBING

0    50    100 km

# Introduction

Golf was not one of the more popular outdoor pastimes in Denmark in the early 1900s, although an 18-hole course was opened in Copenhagen in 1898. With long, hard winters and short daylight hours, such golf as there was was seasonal and the average Dane spent a great deal of his leisure hours on the ski slopes and the ice hockey rinks.

The Aalborg Club was opened in 1908 and had a full and enthusiastic membership but, as one Dane explained to me, the golf clubs were confined to the store-shed during the winter months and only brought out again in the spring of each year when, he went on, 'One had forgotten most of what we learned from the summer before and had to start all over again.'

The majority of the club professionals were from the United Kingdom and they were retained on a seasonal basis only. At the start of each season golf lessons were at a premium and rusty swings and faulty techniques were rectified, only to be put back in moth balls with the advent of winter.

There are now some 39 courses in Denmark, fifteen of which are 9-hole affairs and others of which are either 12, or, in some cases, only six holes. At the last count there were fifteen 18-hole courses with a couple more in the construction stage.

# Selected Courses

## Fano

**Location:** Off the coast of Jutland, reached by ferry from Esbjerg.
**Telephone:** (05) 163282.
**Length:** 4642 metres.
**SSS:** 65.

## Esbjerg

**Location:** Fifteen kilometres north of Esbjerg.
**Telephone:** (05) 269219.
**Length:** 5728 metres.
**SSS:** 70.

## Storstrommen

**Location:** At Falster, fifteen kilometres north of Nykobing.
**Telephone:** (03) 838080.
**Length:** 5945 metres.
**SSS:** 72.

## Helsingor

**Location:** About two kilometres from Helsingor.
**Telephone:** (03) 212970.
**Length:** 6100 yards.
**SSS:** 70.

## Hillerod

**Location:** One kilometre from Hillerod.
**Telephone:** (03) 265046.
**Length:** 5385 metres.
**SSS:** 69.

## Holstebro

**Location:** Thirteen kilometres west of Holstebro.
**Telephone:** (07) 485155.
**Length:** 6505 yards.
**SSS:** 71.

## Kolding

**Location:** Three kilometres from Kolding.
**Telephone:** (05) 523793.
**Length:** 5354 metres.
**SSS:** 68.

## Ringsted

**Location:** Thirty kilometres from Copenhagen.
**Telephone:** (02) 863444.
**Length:** 28 holes, 5893 metres.
**SSS:** 72.

# Copenhagen

**Location:** Thirteen kilometres north of Copenhagen.
**Telephone:** (01) 630483.
**Length:** 18 holes, 5876 metres.
**SSS:** 69.

# SWEDEN

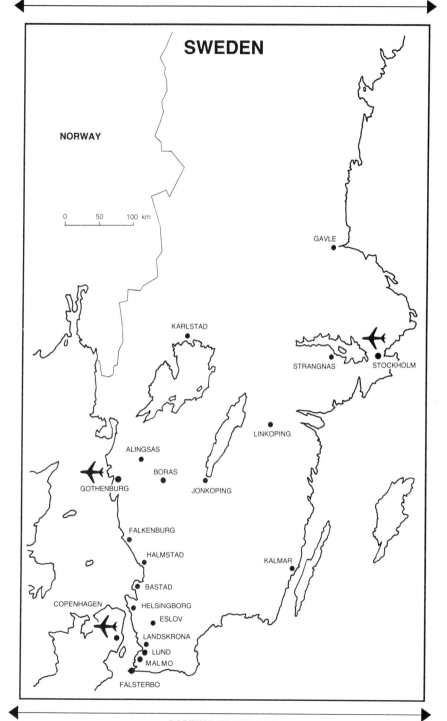

# Introduction

The development of golf in Sweden was a leisurely affair and started around the turn of the century. Hovas, near Gothenburg, was one of the earliest courses but the first 18-hole course was not built until 1929 and as recently as 1945 there were only twenty-two listed golf clubs. Now there are over 120 courses and, at the last count, some 55,000 golfers.

In the last few years, as the dominance of European golf has manifested itself, there has been a renewed interest in golf in Sweden. Several young Swedish professionals are knocking on the doors of high honours in the game and a couple are within striking distance of places in the Ryder Cup team. Winter golf in Spain has its share of sun-seeking Swedish golfers who wish to continue their golf through what can be virtually a closed season in their own country and both amateurs and professionals are very competitive.

# Selected Courses

## Falsterbo

This is the only true links course in Sweden and is one of the finest examples on the Continent. It is laid out on the tip of a peninsula in the southernmost corner of Sweden and whilst Stockholm is some 300 miles to the north-east, Copenhagen is only about 29 miles away, as the crow flies, across the Öresund.

Like all links courses it presents a different challenge on each hole in a matter of hours as the wind changes from gentle breezes off the land to the stiff salt-laden blows from the Baltic. The severe challenge of Falsterbo starts at the dog-leg 1st hole, with out of bounds on the right, and the next four holes, because of their low-lying position, have an abundance of tall marsh-grasses that blend with, rather than indicate, the edges of the water hazards. The 3rd is the only par 5 on the outward nine and is a true three-shotter, and around the side of the 6th are some of the few trees that one encounters on the course. And whilst there are many bunkers on the course it is mainly water hazards that threaten on the first seven holes.

For a course of this calibre it seems a pity that more use has not been made of its subtle challenges and it is still relatively unknown to professional and amateur alike. In 1963 the men's European Amateur Golf Team Championship was held here and the winning English team was captained by no less a golfer than Michael Bonallack – now Secretary of the Royal and Ancient, St Andrews – and he recently recalled the event as just about the most enjoyable that he had ever known and, he was reported as saying, it was not just because the English team were victorious on that occasion. And as though to confirm the 'family' liking for golf in these parts, Mrs Michael Bonallack has the distinction of winning both the last of the Swedish Ladies' and the first of the Scandinavian Ladies' Championships when the titles were incorporated in 1956.

**Location:** Thirty-five kilometres from Malmo.
**Telephone:** (040) 470078.
**Length:** 6400 yards.
**SSS:** 72.

# Other Places To Play

## Barseback

**Location:** Thirty kilometres from Malmo.
**Telephone:** (046) 75053.
**Length:** 5900 metres.
**SSS:** 71.

## Bastad

**Location:** Four kilometres from Bastad.
**Telephone:** 73136.
**Length:** 5760 metres.
**SSS:** 71.

## Soderasens

**Location:** Billesholm, twenty kilometres from Helsingborg.
**Telephone:** (042) 73337.
**Length:** 18-hole course: 6220 metres. 9-hole course: 1600 metres.
**SSS:** 18-hole course: 72. 9-hole course: 27.

## Boras

**Location:** Six kilometres from Boras.

**Telephone:** (033) 501 42.
**Length:** 5570 metres.
**SSS:** 72.

# Eskilstuna

**Location:** Strangnasvagen.
**Telephone:** (016) 142629.
**Length:** 5620 metres.
**SSS:** 69.

# Eslov

**Location:** Three kilometres south of Eslov.
**Telephone:** (0413) 13494.
**Length:** 5760 metres.
**SSS:** 71.

# Falkenburg

**Location:** Five kilometres south of Falkenburg.
**Telephone:** (0346) 50287, 13863.
**Length:** 5670 metres.
**SSS:** 71.

# Gavle

**Location:** Three kilometres from Gavle.
**Telephone:** (026) 113163.
**Length:** 6219 yards.
**SSS:** 71.

# Albatross

**Location:** Ten kilometres north of Gothenburg.
**Telephone:** (031) 550440.
**Length:** 6020 metres.
**SSS:** 72.

# Gothenburg

**Location:** Eleven kilometres south of Gothenburg.
**Telephone:** (031) 282444.
**Length:** 5935 yards.
**SSS:** 69.

# Delsjo

**Location:** Three kilometres from Gothenburg.
**Telephone:** (031) 406959.
**Length:** 5765 metres
**Par:** 71.

# Oijared

**Location:** Twenty-four kilometres from Alingsas. Two courses.
**Telephone:** (03) 023 0604.
**Length:** First course: 5685 metres. Second course: 5755 metres.
**SSS:** First course: 71. Second course: 71.

# Halmstad

**Location:** Nine kilometres from Halmstad. Two courses.
**Telephone:** (035) 30077.
**Length:** 18-hole course: 5980 metres. 9-hole course: 2765 metres.
**SSS:** 18-hole course: 73. 9-hole course: 36.

# Rya

**Location:** Ten kilometres south of Helsingborg.
**Telephone:** (042) 221082.
**Length:** 5775 metres.
**SSS:** 71.

# Vasatorps

**Location:** Eight kilometres east of Helsingborg.
**Telephone:** (042) 235058.
**Length:** 5775 metres.
**SSS:** 72.

# Jonkoping

**Location:** Three kilometres south of Jonkoping.
**Telephone:** (036) 76567.
**Length:** 6370 yards.
**SSS:** 70.

# Kalmar

**Location:** Nine kilometres from Kalmar.

**Telephone:** (0480) 72111.
**Length:** 5950 metres.
**SSS:** 71.

## Karlstad

**Location:** Eleven kilometres from Karlstad.
**Telephone:** (054) 36406.
**Length:** 5900 metres.
**SSS:** 72.

## Landskrona

**Location:** Three kilometres from Landskrona.
**Telephone:** (0418) 19528.
**Length:** 5730 metres.
**SSS:** 71.

## Linkoping

**Location:** Three kilometres from Linkoping.
**Telephone:** (0120) 11425/14614.
**Length:** 5620 metres.
**SSS:** 71.

## Lunds Akademiska

**Location:** Five kilometres east of Lund.
**Telephone:** (046) 99005.
**Length:** 5700 metres.
**SSS:** 71.

## Bokskogens

**Location:** Fifteen kilometres from Malmo. Two courses.
**Telephone:** (040) 481004.
**Length:** 18-hole course: 6080 metres. 9-hole course: 4380 metres.
**SSS:** 18-hole course: 73. 9-hole course: 37.

## Ljunghusens

**Location:** Thirty kilometres from Malmo. Two courses.
**Telephone:** (040) 450384.
**Length:** 18-hole course: 5945 metres. 9-hole course: 2325 metres.
**SSS:** 18-hole course: 73. 9-hole course: 35.

# Sigtunabygdens

**Location:** Fifty-one kilometres north of Stockholm.
**Telephone:** (0760) 50846.
**Length:** 6140 metres.
**SSS:** 73.

# Djursholms

**Location:** Twelve kilometres from Stockholm. Two courses.
**Telephone:** (08) 7551477.
**Length:** 18-hole course: 5590 metres. 9-hole course: 4690 metres.
**SSS:** 18-hole course: 70. 9-hole course: 64.

# Agesta

**Location:** At South Farsta. Two courses.
**Telephone:** (0864) 5641.
**Length:** 18-hole course: 5735 metres. 9-hole course: 3660 metres.
**SS:** 18-hole course: 71. 9-hole course: 61.

# Lidingo

**Location:** Six kilometres from Stockholm.
**Telephone:** (08) 7657911.
**Length:** 5745 metres.
**SSS:** 71.

# Saltsjobadens

**Location:** Sixteen kilometres from Stockholm.
**Telephone:** (08) 7173319.
**Length:** 5675 metres.
**SSS:** 71.

# Stockholm

**Location:** Seven kilometres from Stockholm.
**Telephone:** (08) 7550031.
**Length:** 5525 metres.
**SSS:** 70.

# Wermido

**Location:** Five kilometres east of Stockholm.

**Telephone:** (0766) 20849.
**Length:** 5705 metres.
**SSS:** 71.

# Viksjo

**Location:** Eighteen kilometres from Stockholm.
**Telephone:** (0758) 16600.
**Length:** 5990 metres.
**SSS:** 71.

# FRANCE

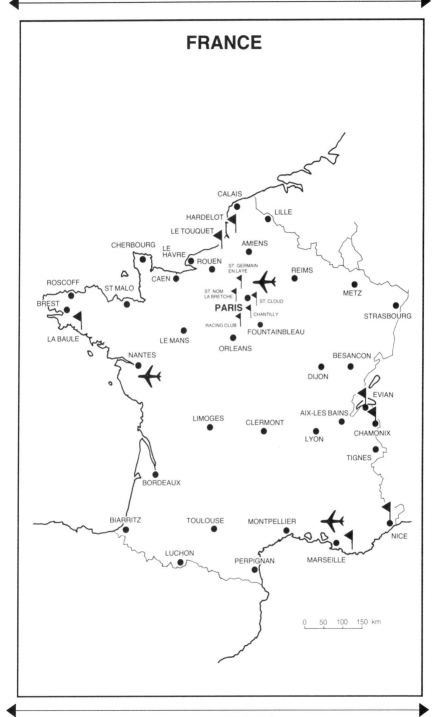

# FRANCE

CALAIS
LILLE
HARDELOT
LE TOUQUET
CHERBOURG
LE HAVRE
AMIENS
ROUEN
ST. GERMAIN EN LAYE
REIMS
ROSCOFF
CAEN
METZ
ST MALO
BREST
ST NOM LA BRETCHE
**PARIS**
ST. CLOUD
STRASBOURG
CHANTILLY
RACING CLUB
LA BAULE
LE MANS
FOUNTAINBLEAU
NANTES
ORLEANS
BESANCON
DIJON
EVIAN
LIMOGES
CLERMONT
AIX-LES-BAINS
CHAMONIX
LYON
TIGNES
BORDEAUX
BIARRITZ
TOULOUSE
MONTPELLIER
NICE
LUCHON
PERPIGNAN
MARSEILLE

0   50   100   150 km

# Introduction

When the Duke of Hamilton and a few of his friends started the Golf Club de Pau in the foothills of the Pyrenees in 1856 it caused about as much comment from the average Frenchman as would the opening of a black pudding factory in Oldham. Golf was hardly known outside Scotland at that time. There were a few golf courses in England and none on the Continent but in the latter years of the nineteenth century the odd course was built in places as far apart as Paris in the north of the country and Cannes in the south.

Between the First and Second World Wars more golf courses appeared but even if the average Parisian was aware of places like St Cloud, Chantilly and St Nom la Breteche, as far as they were concerned it was a game for the ultra-rich. On one of my early visits to the Lancome Trophy which is held at St Nom la Breteche the appearance of Gary Player and Arnold Palmer outside the plush George V Hotel in the heart of the capital did nothing to stimulate the interest of the man in the street. But mention the game of rugby and the conversation became animated.

It is practically impossible to get accurate statistics about all the new courses that are being built but at the last count there are some 196 courses already in France, with 104 under construction, 50 of which were due for completion by 1988. A similar golfing boom took place in Spain in the late 1960s but, unlike Spain, France does not have the same climatic conditions and it is a fact that the holiday golfer is looking for sun as well as golf.

As with all golfing booms it is the development companies that are the prime movers and one such company is building a 'Tournament Players Course' on the lines of the one in America, near Paris, and another development near Cap d' Agde with an 18-hole public course which, the developers say, has been designed to accommodate beginners and average golfers.

Holiday patterns are changing, say the developers, and more people want to play golf on holiday. There is no doubt that the golfing developments in France are aimed at the blossoming tourist market, and that they can only be good for golf.

Do not, under any circumstances, consider purchasing a set of clubs in France unless you came up trumps in the National Lottery the night before, and the same applies to golf balls. A night at the best nightclub in Paris is liable to be cheaper.

# Paris

## Selected Courses

### Chantilly

Chantilly Golf Club was founded in 1908 and five years later the French Open Championship was played there. A second course was commissioned in 1923 and some of the existing holes on the championship course were redesigned. Much of this was destroyed during the Second World War but has since been restored.

There is a feeling of total seclusion at Chantilly and the course provides a challenge to all with its constantly changing character and direction, and whilst there is a premium on accurate driving, the approach shots also demand accuracy if a good score is to be recorded. Peter Oosterhuis retained his French Open title Chantilly in 1974 and can still recall what he described as one of the toughest finishing holes – certainly the longest – in Europe: the 18th at 596 yards.

There are two par 5s on the outward nine, the 8th and the 9th and the 596-yard, par 5 18th but there are also a number of tough, par 4s to contend with.

**Location:** Forty-two kilometres from Paris.
**Telephone:** 44570443.
**Length:** 18-hole course: 7796 yards. 9-hole course: 2625 metres.
**SSS:** 18-hole course: 74. 9-hole course: 34.

### St Cloud

**Location:** Nine kilometres from Paris. Two courses.
**Telephone:** 47010185.
**Length:** First course: 18 holes, 6003 metres. Second course: 18 holes, 5085 metres.
**SSS:** First course: 72. Second course: 68.

### Saint Nom la Breteche

The home of the Lancome Trophy since its inception, this is one of the newer additions to French golf. Both courses are always in first

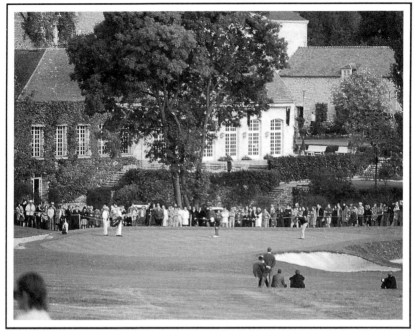

Saint Nom la Breteche – a first-class course with a stylish clubhouse and prosperous membership

class condition and from the forward tees make an ideal holiday golfing venue. The clubhouse is a stylishly converted French farmhouse with an excellent restaurant and all attendant facilities. At the last count the membership was well over one thousand and the majority, as far as I could judge on my last visit, were some of the more wealthy types!

**Location:** Twenty-four kilometres from Paris.
**Telephone:** (1) 34625400.
**Length:** First course: 18 holes, 6684 yards. Second course: 18 holes, 6912 yards.
**SSS:** First course: 72. Second course: 72.

## Racing Club de France, La Boulie

La Boulie was the home of the French Open Championship for a number of years and has two 18-hole and one 9-hole courses. Not too far from the Palace of Versailles it is one of the older developments and has a membership in the region of 1000.

**Location:** Versailles, fifteen kilometres from Paris.
**Telephone:** 9505941.
**Length:** First 18-hole course: 6055 metres. Second 18-hole course: 6206 metres. 9-hole course: 1148 metres.
**SSS:** 72.

## St Germain en Laye

Opened in 1922, St Germain en Laye has an 18 and a 9-hole course. Just off the Route de Poissy and within easy reach of the capital.

**Location:** Twenty kilometres from Paris.
**Telephone:** 4517590.
**Information for Visitors:** Weekend visitors must be accompanied by a member. A telephone call is advisable.
**Length:** 18-hole course: 6115 metres. 9-hole course: 2030 metres.
**SSS:** 18-hole course: 72. 9-hole course: 33.

# Le Touquet

## Introduction

The two golf courses at Le Touquet and the one at Hardelot, about twenty minutes away, are among the better known venues to holiday golfers and for those who are not familiar with either, a visit is a must. The Cote d'Opale is a mere 45 minutes by Hovercraft from Dover and Hardelot a 10 minute drive from Boulogne.

## Selected Courses

### Hardelot

This course has been in existence since 1905 and was designed by that old master architect, Tom Simpson who left his mark on other French courses.

It has been said that Hardelot and The Sea course at Le Touquet are two of the finest tests of golf that you are ever likely to play and both have an 'English' feel about them. The course at Hardelot is carved out of a beautiful old pine forest and has seven par 5s, six par 4s and five par 3s. There are many holes that can be described as 'outstanding' and few that one would dismiss with a wave of a 9 iron! The 126-yard 7th is a prime example – miss the green on any side and you will find yourself reaching for a sand iron – whilst the 17th, at 192 yards demands a long, straight iron through a restricted gap and a tee shot that bears the faintest traces of a hook will be punished by a huge drop to the left away from the green.

There are no easy par 5s and the 13th at 550 yards is made the more difficult by a huge bunker which is thoughtfully placed to trap a long drive! And as though that is not enough to deter the chicken-hearted, a lake cuts into the fairway on the right hand side.

But having played your first round at Hardelot the attractive, modern clubhouse serves some excellent food and local wines, and the sports and leisure complex is not easily matched.

**Location:** Fifteen kilometres from Boulogne.
**Telephone:** 21837310.
**Length:** 6547 yards.
**Par:** 74.

## Le Touquet

Le Touquet itself has two courses, The Sea and The Forest.

The Sea course does not, as the name implies, have holes actually by the sea but there is a great feel of some of the Scottish courses about many of the holes and when the wind blows – as it often does – the player who is able to hit low shots and hold them under the wind will find scoring that much less difficult.

It is hard to imagine that two golf courses so close to each other can be so different. The Forest course bears no resemblance to its neighbour but in some ways it has a sneaking affinity with Hardelot. It is not usually in the same pristine condition, but it is also a good and enjoyable test of golf.

**Location:** Two kilometres south of Le Touquet.
**Telephone:** 21052022.
**Length:** The Sea: 5860 metres. The Forest: 5612 metres.
**Par:** The Sea: 74. The Forest: 72.
**Accommodation:** The Le Manior Hotel does duty as clubhouse, restaurant and hotel for both courses. It is on the expensive side but there are many cheaper and acceptable pensions and restaurants within easy reach.

# Brittany

## Introduction

The south-western part of Britanny is well known to wine buffs – Muscadet in particular – but the golf courses are not so renowned. Yet it is a superb holiday venue.

## Selected Courses

### La Bretesche

A very pleasant parkland course in the grounds of the chateau that was once owned by the barons of La Roche, La Bretesche is an ideal holiday golf set-up. The clubhouse, like those on many other French courses, has been tastefully converted to its present use from the original stable block and barns and includes an attractive hotel.

**Location:** Fifty kilometres from Nantes.
**Telephone:** 40883003.
**Length:** 6605 yards.
**Par:** 72.
**Accommodation:** There is a hotel at the clubhouse. There are also self-catering cottages on the course if you don't mind looking after yourself on holiday.

### La Baule

The La Baule Golf and Country Club has been in existence for around ten years and the golf course was designed by Peter Alliss and Dave Thomas. I was acquainted with this development by both Alliss and Thomas whilst we were sharing a drink at La Manga, Spain and they were both at pains to point out that the golf course was specifically designed with the holiday golfer in mind and that is exactly what they have achieved.

It is a mixture of heath and woodland on the first nine holes whilst the back nine are built around a huge lake. The course is well bunkered – although there are none of a penal nature – and some beautiful old trees play their part in making the golfer think first and hit later. It is quite close to the resort of La Baule and but

30 minutes drive from La Bretesche but it is advisable to avoid the months of July and August as this is a popular spot for the French holidaymaker.

**Location:** Five kilometres from La Baule.
**Telephone:** 40604618.
**Length:** 6200 metres.
**SSS:** 72.
**Accommodation:** The course is owned by the Lucien Barriere hotel group and guests in their hotels are offered free golf at La Baule and Bretesche during the months of May and June and September/October. This also includes free entrance to the La Baule Country Club in the town.

# Nantes

The golf course is a pleasant sixteen kilometres from Nantes Airport and is laid out on gently undulating land among well-established trees. Like La Baule, it is a mixture of heathland and forest architecture and was designed by English golf architect Frank Pennink and, like most of his courses, has a greater premium on accuracy than sheer length. It has some splendid short holes on which the holiday golfer is able to maintain his score without too much effort and to relax before tackling the 525-yard par 5 15th.

Visitors are made welcome at Nantes and if, with its feeling of peace and tranquility, it is not recognised as a regular stop for tourists then it should be and I would not hesitate to recommend it to the average family golfer who needs to relax.

**Location:** Sixteen kilometres from Nantes Airport.
**Telephone:** 40632582.
**Length:** 6100 metres.
**Par:** 72.

# Savoie and The Alps

## Selected Courses

### Chamonix

Mention Chamonix and anyone will tell you that it has been famous for its winter sports and mountaineering since the year dot. It has been said that the towering peaks of Mont Blanc provide shelter for its own abominable snowman and viewing the 15,770 feet of snow-covered landscape from the golf course, which is only 1000 feet above sea level, it is easy to understand the legend.

Club de Chamonix was opened in 1934 with a 9-hole layout of around 4732 metres. And although the course is closed for six months out of twelve, it now has an 18-hole layout which was redesigned by no less an architect than that indefatigable, Robert Trent Jones! Who else, you may well ask, would you commission to build a golf course where snow is abundant and land at a premium?

The present course is some five years old and in many respects I would not describe it as one of the best that this world-famous architect has created. And I only say this in view of the fact that there is a distinct flavour of deja vu about it. Small, elevated greens are savagely guarded by water and bunkers that would do credit to Fort Knox and many an American could be forgiven for thinking that he had played a similar course to this back in the United States.

Having said that, it is one of the few golf courses in the world where the playing becomes secondary to the views that confront one on all sides. The sharp, clear mountain air is in itself a powerful stimulant and a golf ball in flight has never looked whiter or more sharply defined against the clumps of dark green trees and the distant troughs and peaks of the lower slopes of the mountains.

The clubhouse is a functional building built out of local pine and has a turf-covered roof whilst the restaurant and bar cater for all tastes and requirements.

**Location:** Two kilometres from Chamonix.
**Telephone:** 50530628.
**Length:** 6088 metres.
**Par:** 72.

Glorious mountain scenery overlooks the course at Club de Chamonix

# Tignes

Another course well worth visiting in the Savoie–Mont-Blanc region is Golf de Tignes, if only for the fact that it is officially the highest course in Europe, at 6400 feet. It only has 9 holes, which are situated on the fringe of the Vanoise National Park between a lake and the lower slopes of the Grand Motte glacier. Scenically, like Chamonix, it is quite stunning and for most, a leisurely nine holes would be accompanied by lots of camera work for the photo album. The golfing season is from the end of June to the middle of September.

**Location:** Le Val Claret, 73320 Tignes, France.
**Telephone:** 76063722.
**Length:** 1 665 metres.
**Par:** 31.

# Aix-les-Bains

Aix, to aching backs and arthritic joints, is synonymous with soothing thermal baths, and the area was a popular one even in Roman times. Golf was originally added to the curative aspects of Aix in 1910. Many doctors actually recommend a leisurely round of golf as a relief for a bad back.

Golf Club Aix-les-Bains is laid out on gently rolling parkland – which may well have been an inducement to the less active – and unlike other courses in this region, is open for play all the year round. It is a relaxing rather than demanding golf course and typifies the best in holiday golf. Such climbs as there are are gentle in nature and most can be played without too many pauses to catch one's second wind.

For a relatively short course it does have two longish par 3s, the 6th at 237 yards and the 9th at 211 yards, but both of these can be the subject of pleasurable discussion in the clubhouse after the game, especially if you have recorded a par on both! The clubhouse has a large restaurant with excellent food and service and views from the bar on the first floor incline one to linger over a gin and tonic.

**Location:** Three kilometres from Aix-les-Bains.
**Telephone:** 79612335.
**Length:** 5600 metres.
**SSS:** 71.

# Useful Information

The majority of golf courses in France are not well signposted and a copy of the Michelin Motoring Atlas, France, is money well spent and is obtainable at major book shops.

## Golf package tour companies

Longshot Golf Holidays (see SPAIN p. 72)

Meridian Golf,
12–16 Dering St,
London, W1R 9AE.
Tel: 01 493 2777.

French Golf Holidays,
P.O. Box 835,
Brentwood,
Essex, CM13 3QQ.
Tel: (0277) 811082.

Golf in France,
69 Avenue Victor Hugo,
75783 Paris 16,
France.
Tel: 010 (33) 45 02 13 55.

Rendezvous France,
Dept. GW1,
Holiday House,
146–148 London Rd,
St Albans.
Herts, AL1 1PQ.
Tel: (0727) 45400.

Le Grand Golf,
383 Chemin de Champraz,
74400 Chamonix Mout-Blanc,
France.
Tel: 010 (33) 50 53 81 32.

Hoverspeed,
Maybrook House,
Queen's Garden,
Dover,
Kent, CT17 9UQ.
Tel: (0304) 240241 or 01 554 7061.

Brittany Ferries,
The Brittany Centre,
Wharf Rd,
Portsmouth, PO2 8RU.
Tel: (0705) 827701.

Golf St Cyprien,
128a Hamlet Court Rd,
Westcliff,
Essex, SS0 7LN.
Tel: (0702) 343381.

# BELGIUM

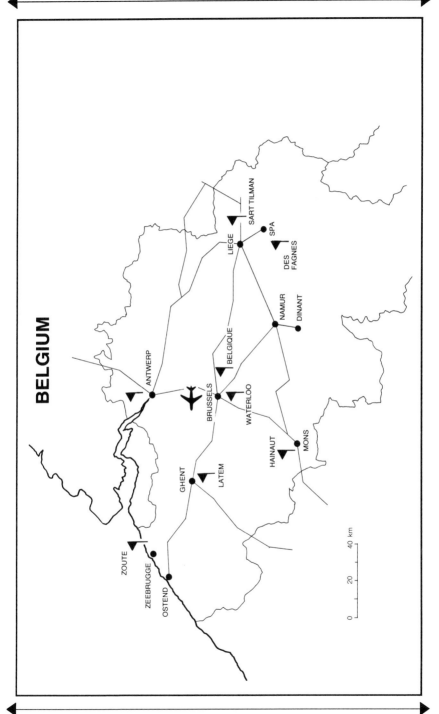

# Introduction

There are twelve golf clubs in Belgium, eight of which had the royal prefix bestowed on them by King Leopold. The oldest of these, Royal Antwerp was founded in 1888, which makes it older than most courses in England. No royal family has taken a keener interest in golf than the Belgian and King Baudouin represented his country in international matches.

# Selected Courses

## Royal Antwerp

Of the twelve clubs possibly the best known is Royal Antwerp. It was formed by members of the local British settlement and the course was first laid out on an army training ground. From this unusual venue a new site was found about seventeen miles from the city and Willie Park was called upon to make the new course. His design remained until the late 1920s when Tom Simpson created the middle ten holes of the main course. Within the main course a shorter nine holes remain which include some of the original Willie Park holes.

Antwerp is a mixture of pine and silver birch trees, heather and shrub, very much after the style of Sunningdale or parts of West Hill and Worplesdon and the similarity does not end there because, like Sunningdale, the course has some very good long par 4s. For the average driver the course is a stiff test of iron play but on many holes even the first-class golfer will be reaching for long irons to the greens. And when one considers that the greens are not large by modern standards the approach shots demand great accuracy. There is a great economy of bunkers, which is typical of the designs of the old school of golf architects, but those bunkers that do exist are placed to catch an off-line shot.

Like many other first-class courses there is not a bad hole as such and the main criticism from the purist's point of view is that the par 5s are not long enough. Having said that I would add that they are quite long enough for the average holiday golfer! The 15th, for instance, requires two big shots whilst a centre fairway bunker on the 5th causes many a bad score.

The course is a riot of colour when the rhododendrons are in flower and in the late summer and early autumn the heather is a beautiful sight.

**Location:** The course is situated some twenty kilometres from Antwerp.
**Telephone:** (031) 668456.
**Length:** 669 yards.
**Par:** 73.

## Royal Golf Club de Belgique

This was the birthplace of Flory Van Donck. One of the older clubs, it was opened in 1902 and has an 18 and a 9-hole course. The 18-hole layout is always in excellent condition and is a first-class test of golf whilst the 9-hole is a tasteful and ideal venue for a few relaxed holes.

**Location:** Fifteen kilometres from Brussels.
**Telephone:** (02) 7675801.
**Length:** 18-hole course: 6200 yards. 9-hole course: 3000 yards.
**Par:** 18-hole course: 73. 9-hole course: 32.

## Royal Waterloo

**Location:** Twenty-two kilometres from Brussels. Two 18-hole courses.
**Telephone:** (02) 6331850.
**Information for Visitors:** It is advisable to telephone before going to the club. A handicap certificate is required before playing.
**Length:** First course: 6260 metres. Second course: 6440 metres.
**SSS:** First course: 73. Second course: 72.

## Royal Golf Club des Fagnes

Another fine golf course which winds its way through the Ardennes forest and is a fine examination of golf.

**Location:** About five kilometres from Spa.
**Telephone:** (087) 771613.
**Length:** 18 holes, 5924 metres.
**SSS:** 72.

# Royal Ostend

**Location:** Seven kilometres from Ostend.
**Telephone:** (059) 233283.
**Length:** 18 holes, 5422 metres.
**SSS:** 70.

# Royal Zoute

Two 18-hole courses that were regularly used by the Belgian royal family. This really is a splendid links layout in every respect and is well worth a visit.

**Location:** One kilometre from Knokke le Zoute.
**Telephone:** (050) 61617.
**Length:** First course: 6131 metres. Second course: 3845 metres.
**SSS:** First course: 72. Second course: 64.

# Royal Golf Club du Hainaut

Was opened in 1934 and although a trifle on the short side is a first class and enjoyable test of golf.

**Location:** Six kilometres from Mons.
**Telephone:** (065) 229610/229474.
**Length:** 5559 metres.
**SSS:** 69.

# Royal Golf Club du Sart Tilman

**Location:** Ten kilometres from Liege.
**Telephone:** (021) 362021.
**Length:** 18 holes, 6013 metres.
**SSS:** 72.

# Royal Latem

**Location:** Ten kilometres from Ghent.
**Telephone:** (091) 825411.
**Length:** 5760 metres.
**SSS:** 70.

# Club du Chateau Royal d'Ardenne

A most pleasant course for a leisurely round of golf.
**Location:** Nine kilometres from Dinant.
**Telephone:** (082) 66628.
**Length:** 5313 metres.
**SSS:** 69.

# HOLLAND

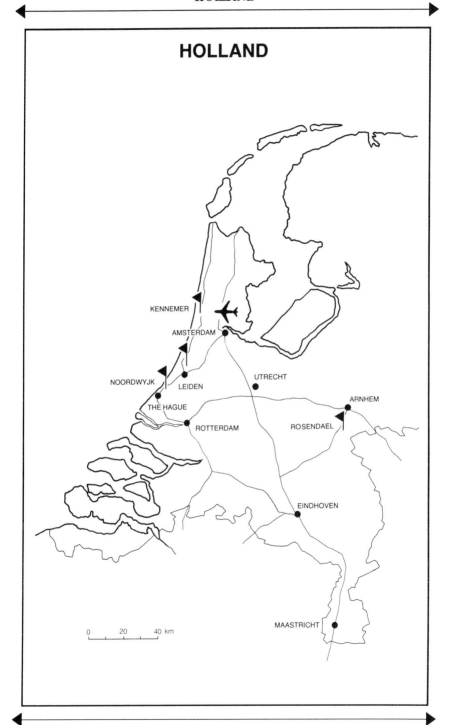

# HOLLAND

KENNEMER

AMSTERDAM

NOORDWYJK

LEIDEN

UTRECHT

ARNHEM

THE HAGUE

ROTTERDAM

ROSENDAEL

EINDHOVEN

MAASTRICHT

0   20   40 km

# Introduction

There are many who say that the game of golf originated not in Scotland but in Holland and to support that claim they refer to a painting by a seventeenth-century Dutchman, Adrien van de Velde which shows their game of kolven – normally played indoors – being adapted to play on ice. The precise origin will probably remain a talking point wherever ardent golfing historians gather. It will never be resolved, I fear, but it is a fact that golf in Holland grew rapidly between the two world wars and that there are now some 22 golf courses in the country, nine of which are 9-hole layouts.

# Selected Courses

## The Hague

The Haagsche Golf Club was opened in 1893 and at the last count had the largest membership in Holland with some 1400 members. It is possibly the most exclusive club in the country.

**Location:** Six kilometres from The Hague.
**Telephone:** (01751) 79607.
**Information for Visitors:** Non-members may only play with an introduction.
**Length:** 6076 yards.
**SSS:** 70.

## Kennemer

Originally founded in 1910, this club was transferred to its present location during the late 1920s and has often been described as among the top twenty in the world.

One could say that it is a great links course but the purists will say that the true links courses have no trees to speak of. Kennemer has beautiful fairways, enormous sandhills and stands of pine trees and the two loops of nine holes start and end where most good courses do, outside the clubhouse. The club has hosted the Dutch Open Championship on many occasions and I have no doubt that it will be the venue for many more.

The circumspect driver will not fear the rough as the fairways are wide and inviting and the greens, which are large, are true and rewarding to the bold putter. There are many lovely holes and some of the carries from the tee are longer than they look at first sight, but from the forward tees the holiday golfer will find all that he requires to test his skill.

David Thomas – a mighty hitter in his competitive days – remembers this lovely course with a deal of affection as he won the 1958 Dutch Open with a total of 277, five strokes ahead of Peter Thompson the Australian, who had beaten him in a play-off for the British Open just previously.

A visit to Holland would not be complete without a round at Kennemer and when you play there, spare a thought for a golfing Canadian colonel who saw fit to demolish the huge, concrete anti-tank wall that practically obliterated the course during the Second World War. From that date onwards all signs of what had been a defence zone vanished – hopefully, never to return – and the course is back to its very best.

**Location:** Six kilometres from Haarlem.
**Telephone:** (02507) 2836.
**Length:** 5860 metres.
**SSS:** 72.

## Amsterdam

An 18-hole course which will provide you with some challenging and worthwhile golf.

**Location:** Eight kilometres from Amsterdam.
**Telephone:** (020) 943650.
**Information for Visitors:** Visitors are welcome, but the fees are a little higher at weekends.
**Length:** 5841 metres.
**SSS:** 69.

## Rosendael

Established in 1896, this is another delightful golf course that provides a good test for all handicaps.

**Location:** Five kilometres from Arnhem.
**Telephone:** (085) 421438.

**Information for Visitors:** Visitors welcome.
**Length:** 18 holes, 6063 metres.
**SSS:** 72.

## Noordwyjk

Another well-established club that was opened in 1922. It has a large and enthusiastic membership of about 900.

**Location:** 15 kilometres from Leiden.
**Telephone:** (025) 233761.
**Information for Visitors:** Visitors welcome.
**Length:** 6040 metres.
**SSS:** 73.

# GERMANY

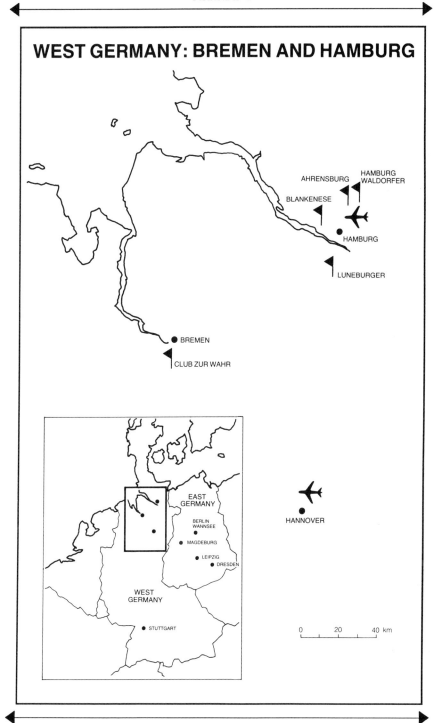

# WEST GERMANY: BREMEN AND HAMBURG

AHRENSBURG    HAMBURG WALDORFER

BLANKENESE

HAMBURG

LUNEBURGER

BREMEN

CLUB ZUR WAHR

EAST GERMANY

BERLIN WANNSEE

MAGDEBURG

LEIPZIG
DRESDEN

HANNOVER

WEST GERMANY

STUTTGART

0     20     40 km

# Introduction

Golf has never had the mass appeal in Germany it has in other parts of Europe, despite early encouragement from the Kaiser who even gave some royal land on which to build new courses. Two of the oldest clubs are the Wiesbadener Golf Club, Wiesbaden, and the Golf and Land Club, Berlin-Wannsee, both of which were opened in 1895. The Homburger Golf Club, Bad Homburg, was opened in 1899 and owed a great deal of its popularity to the Bad Homburg spa.

From the early days there was a slow increase in courses until in 1939 there were fifty. No more were constructed until after the end of the Second World War when a small 9-hole layout was built for the US forces. This 2781-metre course was located near Dachau – a spot that had had more unpleasant associations – and was called the Riverside Golf and Country Club. It was opened in 1947. Several other courses were built specifically for the British and American armed forces. But despite this imported interest in golf and the emergence of Bernhard Langer as a world-class golfer, golf has never taken on in any major way.

The biggest number of golf clubs in one area are the six courses around Hamburg.

# Selected Courses

## Hamburger

Opened in 1906, this is one of the more popular clubs in this region with some 900 members, and is a good test of golf.

**Location:** Blankenese, fourteen kilometres from Hamburg.
**Telephone:** (040) 812117.
**Length:** 18 holes, 6000 metres.
**SSS:** 71.

## Hamburg-Ahrensburg

This club has a membership of around 750 keen golfers and the 18-hole course is a short and pleasant drive from the city.

**Location:** Twenty kilometres from Hamburg city centre.
**Telephone:** (041 02) 56532.
**Length:** 5925 metres.
**SSS:** 71.

## Hamburg Waldorfer

Yet another well-supported club and popular with the local golfers, it has a membership of some 700 and can bring out the best in most classes of golfer.

**Location:** Twenty-one kilometres from Hamburg centre.
**Telephone:** Hamburg 6051 337.
**Length:** 18 holes, 6300 metres.
**SSS:** 72.

## Auf der Wendlohe

This ⁷ 8-hole course had four British professionals when I was last in the area and is a very busy course at most times.

**Location:** Fifteen kilometres from Hamburg city centre.
**Telephone:** Hamburg 5505454.
**Length:** 6060 metres.
**SSS:** 72.

## Hamburger Golf Club in der Luneburger Heide

This was opened for play in 1957 and has a membership of around 600. It is a well-maintained and popular course and well used at weekends.

**Location:** Twenty-five kilometres from Hamburg.
**Telephone:** Hittfeld 041 052331
**Length:** 18 holes, 5865 metres.
**SSS:** 71.

## Bremen

One of the oldest golf clubs in Germany, Bremen was founded in the late nineteenth century as a 9-hole layout but the championship course at Garlstedter Heath owes its existence to the Club Zur Vahr which has a number of sporting and social activities under its corporate title.

The course is dominated by tall pine trees which line the holes from tee to green and from the championship tees it measures 7240 yards with six of the eighteen holes over 500 yards. Designed by Bernard von Limburger it occupies 220 acres of thickly wooded ground and with the number of established trees at his disposal the architect was able to incorporate a great many of them as natural hazards and eliminate the need for too many bunkers. Most of the holes are narrow with sharp dog-legs but most offer a choice of routes to the green.

Neil Coles, who won the German Open in 1971, said that he rated Club Zur Vahr as one of the best championship courses he had played in Europe. Club Zur Vahr is a big course and is for the good driver. There are many holes where the driver must be used because the length is necessary and with the tall trees on either side the tee shot becomes more difficult. But having said that, the premium is on accuracy rather than sheer length if one is to score well at Club Zur Vahr.

The 9-hole course at Bremen Vahr is a pleasant and satisfying one if not as tough as the 18-hole challenge at Garlstedt.

**Location:** Club Zur Vahr: Garlstedter Heath. 9-hole course: within the 18-hole layout.
**Telephone:** 230615.
**Length:** Club Zur Vahr: 6435 metres. Bremen Vahr: 6060 metres.
**SSS:** Club Zur Vahr: 75. Bremen Vahr: 72.

# ITALY

Al Atkinson
Chaytow  0181 568-5688

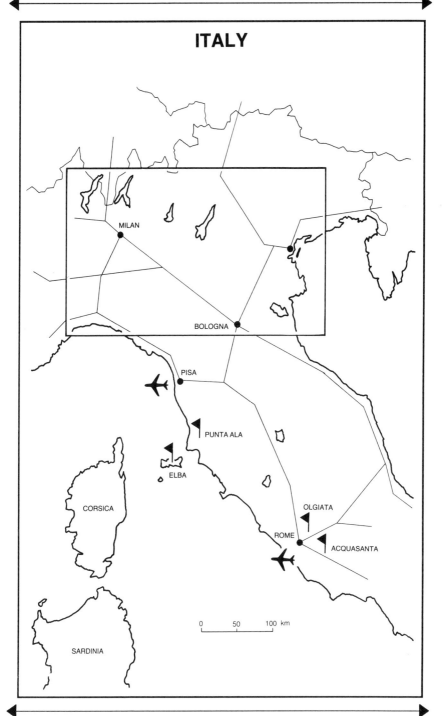

**ITALY**

MILAN

BOLOGNA

PISA

PUNTA ALA

ELBA

CORSICA

OLGIATA

ROME

ACQUASANTA

SARDINIA

0   50   100 km

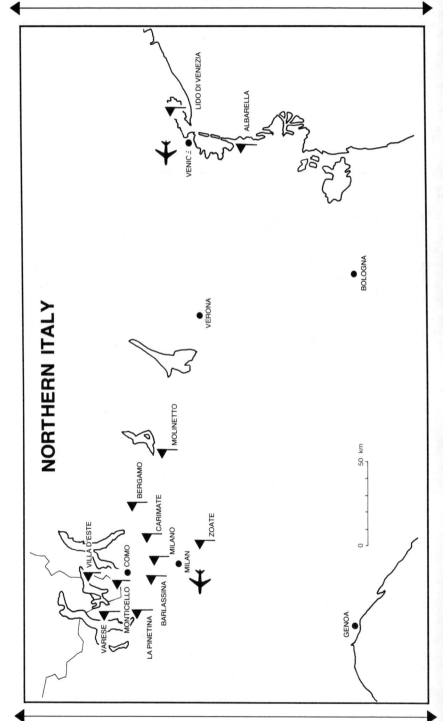

**NORTHERN ITALY**

LIDO DI VENEZIA

ALBARELLA

VENICE

BOLOGNA

VERONA

MOLINETTO

BERGAMO

CARIMATE

VILLA D'ESTE

ZOATE

COMO

MILANO

MILAN

MONTICELLO

BARLASSINA

VARESE

LA PINETINA

GENOA

50 km

0

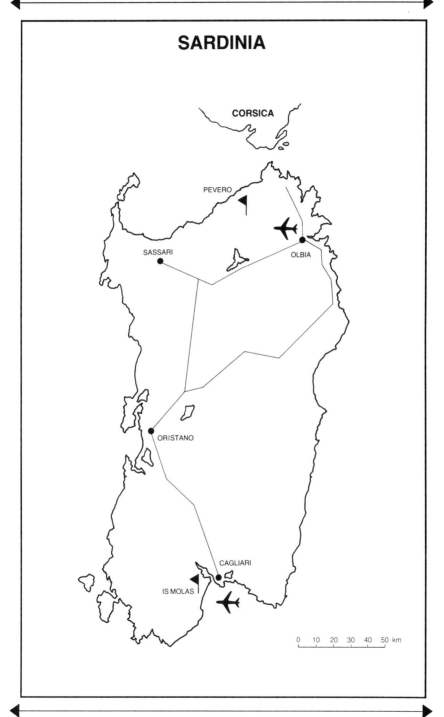

# SARDINIA

**CORSICA**

PEVERO

SASSARI

OLBIA

ORISTANO

CAGLIARI

IS MOLAS

0  10  20  30  40  50 km

# Introduction

One of the first golf courses in Italy, the Circolo del Golf di Roma, was opened in 1903 and other, less significant courses were constructed like the Campo Carlo Magno Golf Club, a 9-hole course which was opened in 1922. A number of other courses were built after this date but interest in golf was limited, fees were relatively high and the average Italian was not interested. The majority of the golf courses which now exist were constructed after the Second World War and there are 34 9-hole courses and 36 18-hole layouts throughout the country. Golf in Italy has attracted thousands of golfers from northern Europe in the past twenty years or so but until recently its courses have not been as well used as those of Spain and Portugal. Now, with the inclusive package golf tours on offer, Italy can offer excellent golf at realistic and affordable prices. Having said that I should point out that practically all of these courses restrict the visitor to weekday rounds, but have the advantage that during the week the courses are relatively empty.

# Milan

## Introduction

If Rome was the site of one of the original clubs there are now 10 clubs within fifty kilometres of Milan, which makes this area the ideal venue for the holiday golfer who wishes to play a number and variety of courses from a base in this cosmopolitan city. There are a number of first-class hotels in Milan which are included in the package deals and for the opera buffs, the added attraction of a night at the world famous La Scala.

## Selected Courses

### Villa d'Este

One of the oldest clubs in this area which was opened in 1926, it is a tough and picturesque course on the banks of Lake Montoferano. It is open from April to November.

**Location:** Forty kilometres from Milan, seven kilometres from Como.
**Telephone:** (031) 200200/200010.
**Length:** 5585 metres.
**Par:** 69.

## Monticello

Opened in 1975 and one of the more popular clubs in this area, Monticello has two courses. It is open from March to December.

**Location:** Forty-five kilometres from Milan, ten kilometres from Como.
**Telephone:** (031) 928055.
**Length:** First course: 6413 metres. Second course: 6056 metres.
**SSS:** First course: 72. Second course: 72.

## Molinetto

An outstanding and enjoyable course, open all year round with exception of August.

**Location:** Seven kilometres from Milan.
**Telephone:** (02) 9238500/9249373.
**Length:** 5823 metres.
**Par:** 72.

## Bergamo

Bergamo L'Albenza Golf Club was opened in 1960 and is the most delightful course. It is open from February to November.

**Location:** Forty kilometres from Milan, thirteen kilometres from Bergamo.
**Telephone:** (035) 640028.
**Length:** 6235 metres.
**Par:** 72.

## Barlassina

Barlassina Country Club was opened in 1957 and is always in good condition. It is open from March to June and then closed until September. It is open again from September to November.

**Location:** Twenty kilometres from Milan, twenty-two kilometres from Como.
**Telephone:** (0362) 560621/560623.
**Length:** 5929 metres.

# Milano

Milano Golf Club was opened in 1928 and is set in La Monza Park. One of the better known clubs in the country it has hosted international tournaments and is always in excellent condition. It is justifiably rated amongst the top five courses in Italy. Both the 18-hole course and the 9-hole course are of championship quality. It is open all year round.

**Location:** Seventeen kilometres from Milan.
**Telephone:** (039) 703081.
**Length:** 18-hole course: 6077 metres. 9-hole course: 2992 metres.
**SSS:** 18-hole course: 72. 9-hole course: 36.

# Varese

Varese was opened in 1934 and has around 500 members. It is a most enjoyable test of golf. The course is closed on Mondays and the season is from March to October.

**Location:** Fifty kilometres from Milan, three kilometres from Varese.
**Telephone:** (0332) 227394/229302.
**Length:** 5860 metres.
**SSS:** 71.

# Carimate

Carimate was opened in 1962 and is an ideal holiday golf course for the medium handicappers. It is open from March to December.

**Location:** Twenty-five kilometres from Milan, seventeen kilometres from Como.
**Telephone:** (031) 790226.

# La Pinetina

An attractive course which will suit the holiday golfer. Open from April to December.

**Location:** Twenty-five kilometres from Milan.
**Telephone:** (031) 930931.
**Length:** 6002 metres.
**Par:** 71.

## Zoate
Another fairly easy course which will suit the casual golfer.

**Location:** Seventeen kilometres from Milan.
**Telephone:** (02) 9060015/9060036.
**Length:** 616 metres.
**Par:** 72.

# Venice

## Introduction

There are three golf courses around the ancient city of Venice to complement the obvious attractions of St Mark's Square, the Grand Canal and the numerous museums and art galleries. The crowded cafes and some first-class hotels make this an ideal spot to combine golf with a little sightseeing.

## Selected Courses

### Lido di Venezia

This championship layout was opened in 1928 and has hosted many international events including the Italian Open and the Italian Amateur Championships. The greens are surrounded by an attractive mixture of trees which include olive, pine and poplar. It is open from March to October.

**Location:** Ten kilometres from the Venice Lido.
**Telephone:** (041) 731015.
**Length:** 6138 metres.
**SSS:** 72.

### Albarella

Albarella is an island that is probably best known to nature lovers and the golf course is situated near the mouth of the river Po.

Opened about 10 years ago it has not yet been accorded the recognition that it deserves. It is a course of great scenic beauty and provides a stern challenge to the best of golfers, especially when the wind is blowing off the sea. It is open from March to November.

**Location:** Fifty kilometres from Venice.
**Telephone:** (0426) 67077.
**Length:** 6085 metres.
**Par:** 72.

# Tuscany

## Selected Courses

### Punta Ala

Punta Ala Golf Club was opened in 1964 and is about a drive and a long iron from the ancient archeological sites of Etruscan Tuscany. Possibly one of the most scenically stunning golf courses in Italy, it wanders through pine and fig trees down to the Mediterranean. The Punta Ala is one of Italy's premier resorts with a selection of night-clubs, restaurants and bars that will refresh the weary golfer.

The course will test any golfer, especially when the wind is blowing off the sea and great use has been made of the many trees both as actual and as line-of-sight hazards. It is an ideal location for the golfer who wishes to spend a part of his holiday taking in the local culture, with the island of Elba a pleasant ferry ride away. It is open all year.

**Location:** Forty-three kilometres west of Grosseto.
**Telephone:** 922121.
**Length:** 6040 metres.
**Par:** 72.

### Elba

For the more adventurous there is a small 9-hole course on Elba – Napoleon's prison exile – and the best pizzas I have every tasted in the little village of Portoferraio, a wedge shot from the forbidding prison which overlooks the small harbour.

**Location:** Portoferraio.
**Telephone:** 966212.
**Length:** 2671 metres.
**Par:** 34.

# Rome

## Selected Courses

### Circolo Golf Olgiata

Designed by the British architect C. K. Cotton in an area that was famous for its Dormello-Olgiata stables, this course was opened in 1961. The 18-hole course is considered by many to rank with some of the finest golf courses in the world and whilst I do not entirely agree, it is a classic golf course with an agreeable overall impression of unlimited space.

Olgiata is a driver's course and there is hardly a straight hole but, having said that, well-placed bunkers demand equally accurate shots to the large greens. Most of the fairway bunkers are beyond the reach of mere hackers and for the holiday golfer, the course is the more pleasant because of that. There are many varied and subtle changes of level but again, Cotton obviously had the handicap golfer in mind by allowing room for alternative shots to be played away from the major hazards.

As a rest from the rigours of the championship course the 9-hole layout is quite delightful, as is the elegant clubhouse which cleverly conceals its size by architecture based on the American ranch style and blends with the surrounding landscape.

The course is open all year.

**Location:** Nineteen kilometres from Rome on the Via Cassia.
**Telephone:** 3788040.
**Length:** 18-hole course: 6862 yards. 9-hole course: 2950 yards.
**SSS:** 18-hole course: 72. 9-hole course: 71.

### Rome (Acquasanta)

Considered to be one of the most exclusive clubs in Italy, Acquasanta lies close to the Appian Way by the Acquasanta Spring, the most unique of settings. A long golf course, it requires accurate hitting at all times and will test the very best of golfers, more especially when the wind is blowing from the west, off the sea. It is open all year.

**Location:** Seventeen kilometres south of Rome on the Appian Way.
**Telephone:** 783407.
**Length:** 5854 metres.
**Par:** 71.

# Sardinia

## Introduction

The island of Sardinia, some 115 miles from Rome and about 120 miles north of the African coast is not immediately associated with holiday golf and its geographical location is such that it has not attracted the popular tour operators. It does, however, have a fine choice of seafood, game and some good wines, dazzling beaches and the most restful atmosphere of any holiday resort I have visited.

The landscape is not conducive to most forms of agriculture and in the north consists of rocky terrain and acres of wild scrub. And whilst there is no denying the aesthetic beauty of the many coves and inlets, at first sight it is not the kind of spot that one would regard as a likely place to build a golf course.

## Selected Courses

### Pevero

It has been said that all one has to do in the Palm Springs area of America is throw a handful of grass seed down, sprinkle it with water and jump back as the grass grows but no such imaginative agriculture existed in Sardinia when that master architect, Robert Trent Jones, was commissioned to build an 18-hole golf course between the savage outcrops of granite, fierce scrub and rising hills that were a natural reserve for predatory foxes and other wildlife. Pevero golf course, in the opinion of its designer, was possibly one of his finest creations. It really is a masterpiece among golf course design. When it was completed it looked so much a part of the

Pevero – a magnificent course wrested from a difficult terrain

surrounding terrain that one had the impression that it had been there from the dawn of time.

Each hole at Pevero is a separate experience and whilst the fairways are generously wide the rough is penal and any shot that misses the fairway usually results in a lost ball. There are many memorable holes at Pevero and the casual golfer can often find himself distracted by differing views as the course winds its way through the dramatic landscape. The most striking view of all, in my opinion, is from the 4th tee, where the ground drops down towards the distant green some 388 yards away and the backcloth to this consists of the emerald green waters of the Bay of Pevero and the snow-clad hills of the island of Corsica in the distance.

There is an ample supply of electric golf carts, trolleys and clubs for hire and at nearby Cervo there is an extensive sports centre. And when you have sampled all the delights of Pevero and the surrounding area a trip to the southern tip of the island, either by air from Olbia Airport or by hire car is well worth while.

**Location:** Costa Smeralda.
**Telephone:** (0789) 96072.
**Length:** 6800 yards.
**Par:** 72.

**Accommodation:** The Hotel Cala di Volpe is only 250 yards from the 16th tee and were I asked to give this establishment a star rating it would be 10. Having said that, it is very expensive and an ideal place to stay if you have won the pools! Accommodation, food and service are without peer but there are two less expensive hotels: the Cervo and Pitrizza hotels which are only a ten minute drive from the golf course and very good value.

## Is Molas

This course was opened in 1975 and is quite close to Cagliari. There are direct flights from the Italian mainland as there are to Olbia in the north.

Is Molas is set on undulating land near the sea although it is not a links course as such. It is a tough test of golf from the back tees but due allowance has been made for the handicap golfer from the forward markers. It was financed by the Bastogi Company whose two chief executives are natives of Sardinia and the golf course is part of a major tourist development in southern Sardinia.

**Accommodation:** The attractive Is Morus Hotel is situated in a secluded spot alongside the sea and the Forte Hotel Village which combines a hotel and a villa complex has around 1600 beds and caters for a variety of tastes and budgets.

**Location:** Five kilometres from Cagliari.
**Telephone:** (070) 92007.
**Length:** 7030 yards.
**Par:** 73.

# Useful Information

Longshot Golf Holidays by Meon offer a package that includes an Alitalia direct flight to Fiumicimo Airport, self-drive car and hotel accommodation.
**Telephone:** (0730) 66561.

# Index